K – 2

Social Studies Alive!®

Solutions for Effective Instruction

A Sourcebook for Building Social Studies Skills, Integrating Language Arts, and Differentiating Instruction

TCi™

Chief Executive Officer: Bert Bower

Chief Operating Officer: Amy Larson

Director of Product Development: Liz Russell

Managing Editor: Laura Alavosus

Project Editor: Carol Domblewski

Editorial Associates: Anna Embree, Sarah Sudano

Production Manager: Lynn Sanchez

Design Manager: Jeff Kelly

Graphic Designer: Victoria Philp

Contributing Writers: Carol Domblewski, Chris Garcia

Photography
Title page:
T: RF/Getty Images
M: Ableimages/Getty Images
B: Elie Bernager/Getty Images

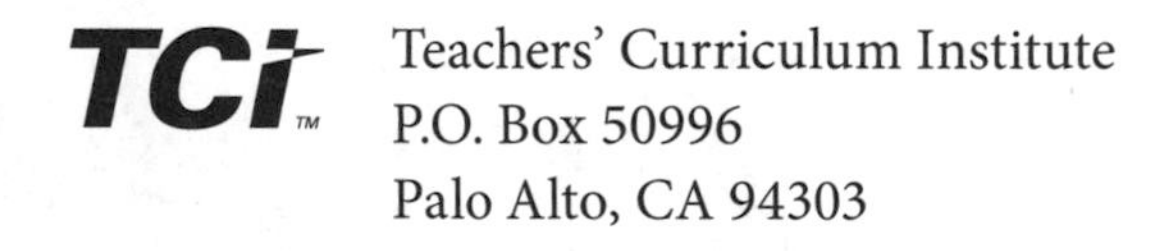
Teachers' Curriculum Institute
P.O. Box 50996
Palo Alto, CA 94303

Customer Service: 800-497-6138
www.teachtci.com

ISBN 978-1-58371-748-6
3 4 5 6 7 8 9 10 -MLI- 15 14 13 12 11 10

Part One

Building Social Studies Skills

Compare and Contrast

The skill of comparing and contrasting helps students examine and gain insight into the people, places, and events in their world and in history. Comparing and contrasting is often a necessary first step in the use of other skills too, such as making decisions.

Teach the Skill Begin by comparing and contrasting something familiar to all students, such as a textbook and a workbook or a lunch box or other lunch carrier and a brown bag. Project *Solutions Master 1: Venn Diagram.* Write the names of the two things you are comparing above the outer circles. Then point to the overlapping area. Explain that this is the place to write how the items are the same. Elicit students' ideas and record them. Next, point out the first large circle and its label. Ask what is different about the first object or item to be compared. Record students' ideas. Then point to the other large circle and its label. Ask what is different about the second object or item to be compared. Record students' ideas. Review what the Venn shows by saying ____ *and* ____ *are alike because* ____, and point to the inner circle as you speak. Then say, ____ *is different from* ____ *because it* ____, and point to the first large circle as you speak. Finally, say, ____ *is different from* ____ *because it* ____, and point to the second large circle as you speak. Fill in the blanks yourself, or have volunteers fill them in for you.

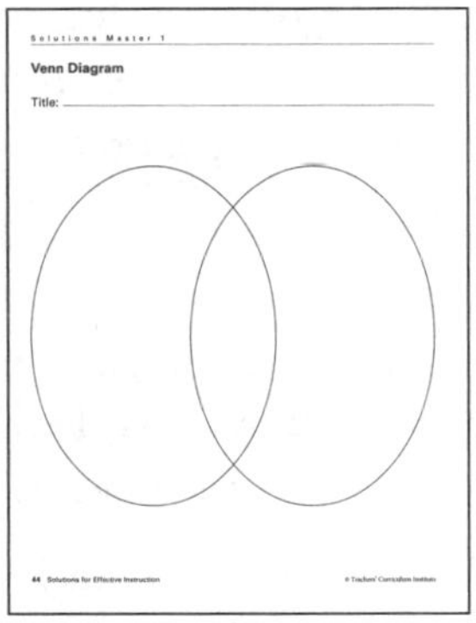

Solutions Master 1: Venn Diagram

Practice the Skill Have students form pairs and distribute copies of *Solutions Master 1: Venn Diagram* to each pair. Ask students to use the diagram to compare and contrast two jobs in your school (such as the jobs of principal and secretary), two places, two events, or two other items you wish to teach, review, or introduce. Ask pairs to begin the work of comparing and contrasting by labeling the two large circles; review their choices. Have students fill in the diagram and, as a class, discuss what their diagrams show.

Classify/Categorize

To classify or categorize is to sort things into groups or to determine a category or categories into which groups of things fit. The skill of classifying sometimes helps students learn how concepts relate to one another; more often, it is a way of demonstrating mastery of concepts. By classifying places, jobs, groups of people, landforms, or events, students can organize their ideas about social studies and create or reinforce links in their semantic or concept maps.

Teach the Skill Tell students that they can classify by sorting things into groups. The groups are called categories. Ask students whether they have ever sorted things into groups. They probably have done so at home when putting dishes away or at school when learning sound and spelling patterns. Tell them there are three simple steps to classify things: *1) Decide how the items are alike and different. 2) Name categories to sort the items into. 3) Place or list the items in the categories.* Write and read two or three classroom rules whose purpose is safety. Then write and read two or three classroom rules that are about being fair. Read the rules aloud. Then project *Solutions Master 2: Two-Column Chart.* Label the columns *Rules for Being Safe* and *Rules for Being Fair.* Explain that these are two categories that students can put the rules in. Ask them for their ideas about where each rule belongs and record the rules. Review what the chart shows.

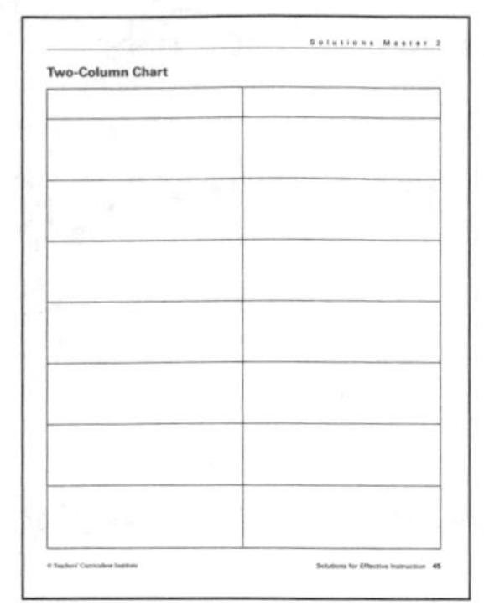

Solutions Master 2: Two-Column Chart

Explain that sometimes classifying things involves looking at related things and naming a category or categories to put them in. For example, review these concepts: sharing, talking, listening, and taking turns. Ask students to name a group into which all these concepts can fit. (One good answer is "ways to get along in school.")

During writing instruction, you can transfer classification and categorization skills to the task of writing paragraphs by noting how the category often becomes part of the topic sentence, while the things that belong in the category often become the supporting sentences.

Practice the Skill Use familiar lesson content for practicing classification or categorization. For example, following a lesson on needs and wants, distribute a variety of pictures from magazines that illustrate needs and wants or list various needs and wants. Ask students to sort the pictures or list the words using those categories. Then distribute copies of *Solutions Master 2: Two-Column Chart,* and have students label the columns and list the items in the correct column. Discuss what their organizers show.

Sequence

Sequencing is putting events in time order. When they sequence, students gain a better understanding of change over time and take a first step toward learning why things happened as they did. Sequencing also deepens students' understanding of the concepts of past, present, and future.

Teach the Skill Tell students that sequence is the order in which things happen. List and display signal words that show a time relationship, such as *at the same time, then, next, after, later, before, first, second, third,* and *last.* Project a paragraph from a chapter you are teaching or a paragraph that is based on content that you are teaching or reviewing, and which shows a sequence of events. Read the paragraph aloud. Read it again slowly. Ask students to raise their hands when they hear a signal word. Underline or circle that word. After reading, project *Solutions Master 3: Sequence Chain.* Ask students, *What happened first?* Record their answer in the first box. Continue by asking what happened next and what happened last, until the sequence is completely recorded. Note that students

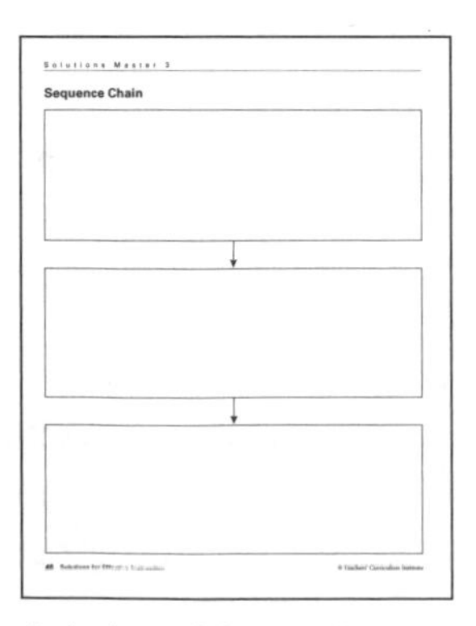

Solutions Master 3: Sequence Chain

can always add more boxes to the sequence chain if they are needed. Review the sequence of events and its time order.

Practice the Skill Project images of three different modes of transportation throughout history onto a screen or write words that name the different modes, such as *horse, train, car, plane,* and *space shuttle.* Distribute copies of *Solutions Master 3: Sequence Chain* to each student, and ask students to sequence them, or put them in time order. Discuss the results. For practice, students might also sequence the events of their school day or events of a favorite holiday.

Identify Cause-and-Effect Relationships

Understanding cause and effect helps students learn why an event happened and the results of that event. Students will use this skill in all strands of social studies. In history, students see the causes of key events and what happened because of those events. Using cause and effect, students can link economic concepts such as workers making goods to people buying the goods, and having a good job to saving money. In geography, identifying cause-and-effect relationships helps students understand concepts such as how landforms affect how people live in and change their environment.

Teach the Skill Present students with some everyday or familiar causes and effects. For example, the school bell rings and everyone gets in their seats. The clock strikes 11:45 and students line up to go to the cafeteria. Project *Solutions Master 4: Cause-and-Effect Diagram* and record one of these simple relationships in the boxes. Note how some causes have just one effect. Then wipe the transparency clean and talk about a cause with more than one effect. For example, if there is an extremely bad storm or a power outage, there may be at least two results: school is closed and students have a day off. Record this example or another example of a single cause with more than one effect. Review what the transparency shows. Write these sentence frames on the board, read them aloud, and ask students to use them to sum up the content of the organizer: *As a result of ____, ____ happened ____ caused ____. The reason why ____ is that ____.*

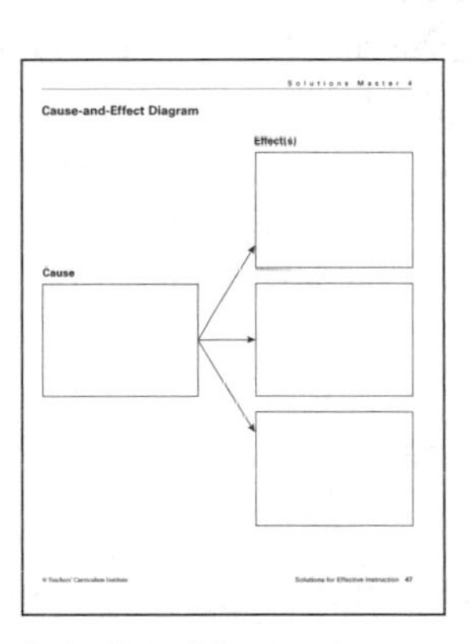

Solutions Master 4: Cause-and-Effect Diagram

Practice the Skill Present a cause and effect or effects that students have read about or discussed recently. For example, say, *Many bike riders are now using busy roads.* Note that this is the cause of problems and changes. Distribute copies of *Solutions Master 4: Cause-and-Effect Diagram* to students. Write *Many bike riders are now using busy roads* in the cause box. Then have students come up with one or more effects of this problem. Discuss their answers, which will vary, and may include new fines for breaking helmet laws, more or different bike laws, a new bike lane or path, or accidents or injuries to riders and walkers. Review how to use the organizer to record effects clearly and correctly, and ask students to sum up what their completed organizer shows.

Analyze

When they analyze, students gain a better understanding of a concept by breaking it down into its parts. Students can use the skill during reading, writing, speaking, listening, and viewing. Often, analysis is a starting point or first step in the use of other skills, such as decision making and evaluation.

Teach the Skill Review a concept you are teaching such as community. Ask what parts make up a community. Students might name places in a community, such as schools, police and fire stations, homes, stores, parks, and places to worship. Students might also name people or groups who make up a community, such as families, city or town workers, health care workers, and others. Project *Solutions Master 5: Web.* Label the center with the concept you are discussing, such as community. Label the secondary circles with the ideas that students have offered. Here, as with other graphic organizers, note that you can add parts, such as circles, if the organizer does not show enough of them, or cross out parts you do not need to use. When you are finished, ask a volunteer to sum up what the organizer shows. Note that students have just analyzed a community. That is, they have just shown some of the parts that make up the whole community.

Solutions Master 5: Web

Practice the Skill Present another concept you are currently studying, such as the environment. Have students form pairs, and distribute copies of *Solutions Master 5: Web* to each pair. Ask them to record the concept in the center of the web. Then ask pairs to work together to name the parts that make up the concept. Have pairs present what their completed organizers show, and reinforce the idea that they have just analyzed the concept by breaking it down into its parts.

Evaluate

When students evaluate, they go beyond just learning from the text and enter into a process of making judgments about what they read. For example, students might evaluate the decisions people made in the past. Another way students can evaluate is by judging how important or interesting ideas or information is to them.

Teach the Skill Invite students to evaluate content you are studying now, such as family traditions, by asking what is familiar or true for them. Present examples of the content, such as this content about holidays and traditions (Grade 1):

Grandparents tell special stories.

Parents teach their students special games.

Parents teach their students how to make special things.

Ask students whether these statements are true for them. Then ask them whether they think these statements are true for other people or help show traditions in other families. Next, ask students to make an evaluative statement about these ideas. To do so, ask,

Are the statements generally right or wrong?

Do the statements do a good job of teaching you about family traditions?

Do the statements help you understand that a tradition is a special way of doing things, and that families have different traditions?

Note that a good reader makes judgments, or evaluates, while reading. Whenever students decide why they did or did not like a book or story, for example, they are evaluating.

Practice the Skill Present students with other content to evaluate, individually or with a partner. Content might come from the same chapter, such as statements about how families celebrate special days (such as with birthday balloons, birthday songs, and piñatas) or from a chapter you wish to review. Ask students to evaluate by thinking about whether the ideas are true for them or true for others. Then ask students to make a decision about whether or how well the content helps them learn about family traditions. Discuss students' evaluations as a class.

Predict

When students predict in social studies, they use their knowledge of a topic, often in combination with events from the past, to offer an informed guess about what might happen next. Logical, thoughtful predictions often rely on the skills of applying and synthesizing knowledge.

Teach the Skill Review, teach, or introduce a lesson by naming behaviors that children know and understand. For example, to introduce or teach "How Do I Make Friends?" (Kindergarten), you might ask students to tell what happened to them in the past when they were nice to their friends. Then ask them to predict what will happen if they are nice again. Use other lesson concepts such as introducing oneself and asking a friend to play to elicit, first, students' prior knowledge of what happened in the past, or a fact about the past, and, second, their prediction of what might happen in the future if they repeat the same behavior or if they do something different. Explain that what happened in the past is a fact that students already know. Point out that students use what they already know to make a prediction when they are reading stories and when they are studying social studies. Project *Solutions Master 6: Prediction/Inference Diagram*. Review the steps in making a prediction by recording one of the examples you just presented, such as being nice to a friend. Label the last box *My Prediction,* and use it to record the students' prediction.

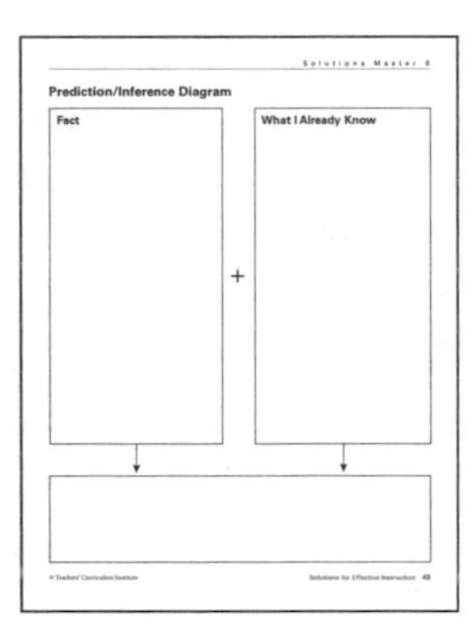

Solutions Master 6: Prediction/Inference Diagram

Practice the Skill Use other lesson content for practicing the skill of making predictions. For example, you might review the chapter content about people around the world (Kindergarten). Ask students to use what they have learned to predict what they would find out or learn if they visited a country they had never visited before. Emphasize how students use what they already know to make their prediction. Distribute copies of *Solutions Master 6: Prediction/Inference Diagram* and have students use it to make and record their predictions.

Make Inferences

Making inferences means reading between the lines. When students make inferences, they arrive at a meaning that is implied in the text but not directly stated there. The skill is closely related to the skill of drawing conclusions in that students must draw on or put together textual information in order to infer. Inferences differ from conclusions, however, in that inferences always require students to use their own prior knowledge or experience. Furthermore, an inference is often based on a single or small bit of information, such as a sentence or two. It is often most useful in telling why. Conclusions, on the other hand, often result from reading longer amounts of text, such as whole sections or chapters. Conclusions often also result from combining textual information without taking personal experience or judgments into account.

Teach the Skill For younger students, inferences are most easily and clearly taught with a narrative rather than with text that explains or persuades. You might use a story that the class has read recently to teach the skill, a true-life story, or a Reading Further selection such as "The Apple Dumpling" (Grade 1). After students have read the story, project *Solutions Master 6: Prediction/Inference Diagram.* Use the first box to record a bit of evidence from which students might make an inference. For example, in "The Apple Dumpling," the woman trades a bag of feathers for her plums, even though the woman wants apples. Then read the label of the next box, *What I Already Know.* Ask students what they think or know about a person who wants or needs one thing but still agrees to take something else for it. Students might say that the woman is nice, or agreeable, or silly, or trusting, or eager to do the right things for her neighbors. They might also say she is an example of how trade sometimes works. Record their answers in the box. Then guide students to make an inference. Label the last box *What I Read Between the Lines* and provide a sentence starter: *The woman in "The Apple Dumpling" is* ____. Have students complete the sentence with words or phrases that describe the woman. Record the inference and explain why it is a good example of reading between the lines: the story does not state this, but it does suggest it. Also explain that the statement is a good example of reading between the lines because students used story details and their own knowledge to come up with the statement.

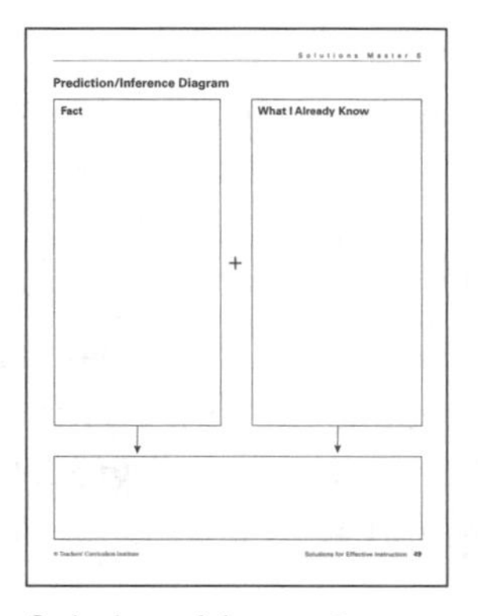

Solutions Master 6: Prediction/Inference Diagram

Practice the Skill Present another example of information from the text from which it is possible to draw an inference, such as the picture and text clues about Betsy Ross (Grade 1). Have students form pairs, and distribute a copy of *Solutions Master 6: Prediction/Inference Diagram* to each pair. Have pairs complete the organizer and share and compare their inference with the inferences of other pairs. Review the process of making inferences or reading between the lines, as well as the results, as a class.

Draw Conclusions

When students draw conclusions, they practice putting ideas and concepts together in order to make a new statement that goes beyond what they learned. Drawing conclusions requires students to read or listen carefully and focus on facts. It often requires them to ask questions about what they are learning; at times, it also requires students to draw on prior knowledge. Drawing conclusions always requires original and critical thinking as students decide how the facts work together to lead to a single statement about their meaning.

Teach the Skill Tell students that a conclusion is an idea that they come to after learning new facts from reading or listening. Explain that, sometimes, their conclusion comes from both those new facts they learn and what they already know. Then, using a lesson you are teaching, introducing, or reviewing, give an example of how students can combine facts with what they already know. Project *Solutions Master 7: Draw-a-Conclusion Diagram*. Ask students for facts about a topic you are studying now. For example, ask for the facts about what good helpers do at school. Students may say, for example, that good helpers at school help clean up, share their books, are careful with crayons and pencils, ask questions, line up for recess, and say *please* and *thank you*. List their ideas in the *Facts* box. Then point to the box labeled *What I Already Know*. Ask students to think about whether they are good helpers at school. Distribute a copy of *Solutions Master 7: Draw-a-Conclusion Diagram* to each student. Have them copy the facts from the transparency. Then, in the next box, have them write the ways in which they are or are not good helpers at school. When they are done, ask them to draw a conclusion about whether they are good helpers. Use the last box on the transparency to record their conclusion, which might say, *I am usually a good helper at school because I help clean up, am careful with crayons and pencils, line up for recess, and say* please *and* thank you.

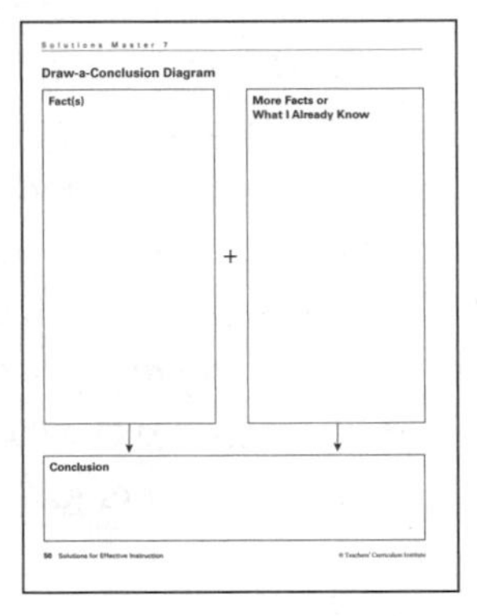

Solutions Master 7: Draw-a-Conclusion Diagram

Practice the Skill Tell students to draw a conclusion about something they already studied or that you have discussed recently as a class. For example, you might ask them whether they would like to be students now or long ago (Grade 1). Have students form pairs, and distribute copies of *Solutions Master 7: Draw-a-Conclusion Diagram* to each pair. Ask students to list facts they already know about school long ago in the Facts box. Have them list their own thoughts about what they prefer in the box labeled *What I Already Know*. Then ask them to draw a conclusion about whether they prefer being students now to being students in the past. As a class, discuss the conclusions and the process of reaching them.

Summarize and Generalize

When students generalize, they put together facts and details they read or learn in order to make an overall, or general, statement about a topic or subject. Generalizing is similar to making inferences and drawing conclusions in that students must synthesize ideas in order to come up with new thinking that is based on, but not directly stated in, the text or in the information they listen to or view. Generalizing also often depends on the skill of summarizing.

Teach the Skill At grades 1 and 2, point out a chapter summary. Explain that these sentences sum up, or briefly tell, what all the chapter content is about. Explain that a summary turns all of the content in a section, chapter, book, or article into one or more statements that tell what it is mainly about.

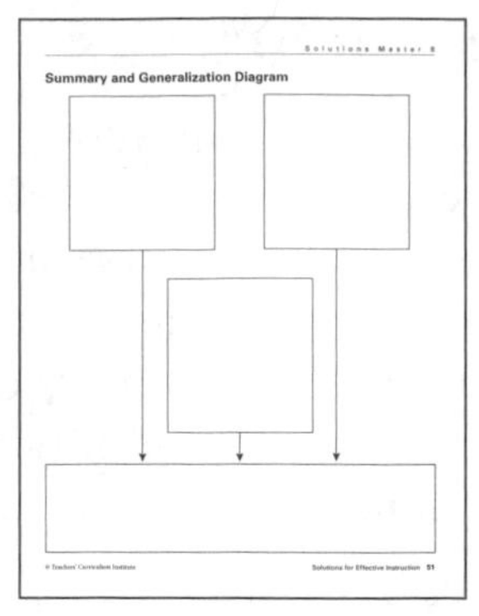

Solutions Master 8: Summary and Generalization Diagram

Project *Solutions Master 8: Summary and Generalization Diagram.* Explain that one way to sum up chapter content is to look at the main headings of the chapter. Ask students to look, for example, at the chapter about maps in Grade 1. Ask them to name all the headings in the chapter, and record them in the top boxes of the diagram. You will need to add a fourth top box; as you add it, note that students can always add or take away boxes, circles, rows and columns, or other parts, from any graphic organizer. Record these phrases derived from the section headings: *drawing of a place, has symbols, has key,* and *has compass rose to show directions.* Then ask students to combine that information into one single statement or other summary, such as, *A map is a drawing of a place that has symbols, a key, and a compass rose to show directions.* Note how this statement sums up the chapter. Record the summary statement in the bottom box. Label it *Summary.* Students might enjoy comparing this summary with the chapter summary.

Explain that students can take a summary statement, or a statement that covers a big topic or subject one step further by making a generalization. Write these sentence starters for generalizations: *Usually,* ____. *Most of the time,* ____. *Many people* ____. *It often happens that* ____. *Most* ____. *All* ____. Explain that generalizations tell what is true all or most of the time and, now that students have studied maps, or another topic, they may be able to make a generalization about it.

Wipe off the content in *Solutions Master 8: Summary and Generalization Diagram.* Tell students that to make a generalization, you will begin with what they learned about maps by studying their chapter, and write the summary statement in one of the top boxes. To help students move beyond the summary to making a reasonable generalization about maps, ask them to look at other maps in your classroom or to tell you what they know about maps. Some might say, for example, that not all maps have a compass rose. Others might say that some maps have colors as well as symbols. They might note that some maps show the world while others show a city or town. Record their ideas in the other top boxes of the transparency. Tell students that to make a generalization, their job is to combine what they have learned from their book with other sources of information. Explain that when people make a generalization in this way, they often end up using words such as *many, most, some,* and *usually.* Occasionally, they use the word *all.* Model a generalization based on the information on the transparency: *Most maps are drawings of a place that have symbols, a key, and a compass rose to show directions,* or *All maps show a place.* Record the generalization in the bottom box of the transparency. Label it *Generalization.* Review what the completed transparency shows, and ask students to tell how summarizing and generalizing are related.

Practice the Skill Have students practice the skill by repeating the summarizing step with another chapter they have already studied. Have students form pairs to record their summary and then to add facts they know or look up from other sources, such as classroom or online reference materials. Then ask them to make a generalization. Discuss the summary statements and generalizations as a class.

Distinguish Fact and Opinion

Understanding the difference between fact and opinion is an important life skill as well as social studies skill. Setting facts apart from opinions helps students decide what information to rely on or trust.

Teach the Skill Write a list of facts and opinions about your classroom. For example, write these statements, and read them aloud to students:

This is the best classroom in our school.

The classroom temperature is 72°F.

There are 26 desks in our classroom.

I think the walls would look better painted blue.

Ask students: *Can you prove that any of these statements are true?* Students might say they can prove it is 72° by looking at the classroom thermostat or by using a thermometer. Note that facts are statements that can be proven true, and explain that students can prove something true by counting, measuring, and so on; by using evidence they see or by observing something; or by finding evidence in reference sources, such as atlases, almanacs, encyclopedias, and so on. Project *Solutions Master 2: Two-Column Chart.* Label the heads *Fact* and *Opinion.* Write the statements about temperature and desks in the *Fact* column. Record the other two statements in the *Opinion* column. Ask students to tell you why these statements are not facts. After students say that the statements cannot be proven true, explain that opinions are statements of belief or feeling. Point out that opinions often contain clue words. Some clue words are action words such as *think, believe,* and *feel.* Other clue words are describing words such as *best, worst, good, okay, bad, lucky, great,* etc. Have students locate examples of these words in the opinion statements you recorded. Circle the words.

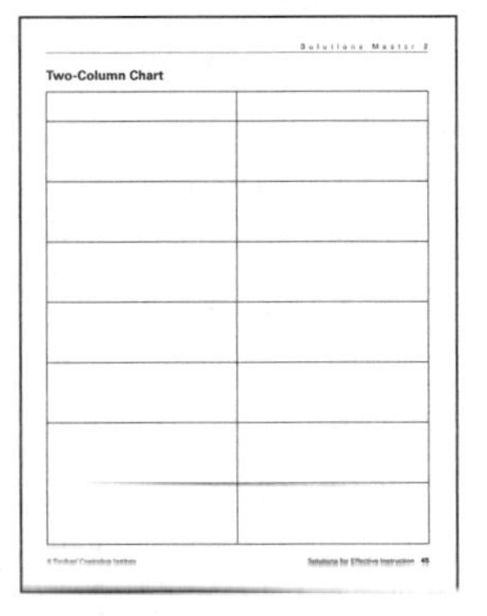

Solutions Master 2: Two-Column Chart

Return to the two-column chart. Draw a thick line under the statements you have already recorded. Ask students to tell you what they have learned about facts and opinions, and use the remaining rows to record the information.

Practice the Skill Give students written text that includes both fact and opinion statements about a topic you are teaching now or wish to review. For example, you might write these statements about school rules:

We have rules at our school.

Rules about being fair are the most important rules.

I think we need new rules for the playground.

One rule in our school is that we can't run in the hall.

Ask students to decide whether the statements are facts or opinions. Remind them that statements of fact can be proven true. Opinions are statements that express a person's belief or feeling. Distribute *Solutions Master 2: Two-Column Chart*, have students label the columns *Fact* and *Opinion*, and ask them to record the statements of fact and opinion in the correct columns of the chart. Also ask them to circle the clue words that tell them that some of the statements are opinions. Discuss their choices.

Support a Position

When students support a position, they tell why they made a certain choice or believe in a certain position or course of action. Supporting a position means giving reasons and explaining them.

Teach the Skill On the board, write and read a sentence frame such as, *I think* ____. Explain that students can complete this sentence by stating a position, or an opinion on an issue. Call on a volunteer to state an opinion on an issue in your school, such as, *I think we should skip spring vacation and get out of school earlier in summer.* Explain that this is the position. Then ask students to name reasons that support the position. For example, students might say that their school could save money on air conditioning. Explain that the reason students give is their support. Have students form pairs, and distribute a copy of *Solutions Master 9: Support Chart* to each pair. Have students work to fill it in together using the opinion above and support generated by the class or other support. Have them summarize what their completed organizer shows.

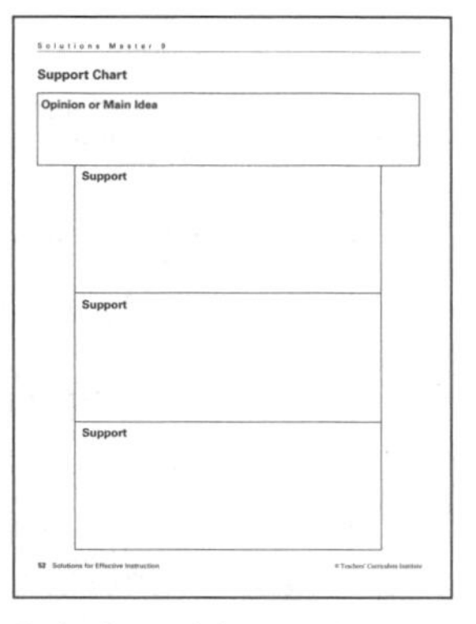
Support Chart

Opinion or Main Idea

Support

Support

Support

Solutions Master 9: Support Chart

Practice the Skill State one pro and one con position related to a topic you are currently studying or an issue in your community. For example, write, *Position 1: Our town needs a dog park/bike path/new school,* and *Position 2: Our town should not spend money on a dog park/bike path/new school.* Divide the class into two teams, pro and con, and ask those teams to divide themselves into small groups of two to three students. Have each small group develop a list of two or more reasons to support the position they were assigned to. Discuss the reasons groups come up with and review the concepts of position (or opinion) and support.

Make Decisions

Students make a decision by choosing between two or more things or two or more courses of action. Using the skill helps students evaluate choices made by people in the past as well as in today's world. Students can apply this skill to the choices they make as students, family members, members of other groups or teams, friends, citizens, and consumers.

Teach the Skill Tell students that making decisions is a process like the writing process: there are steps to follow. Usually, students follow the steps in a certain order, although sometimes they must go back to an earlier step.

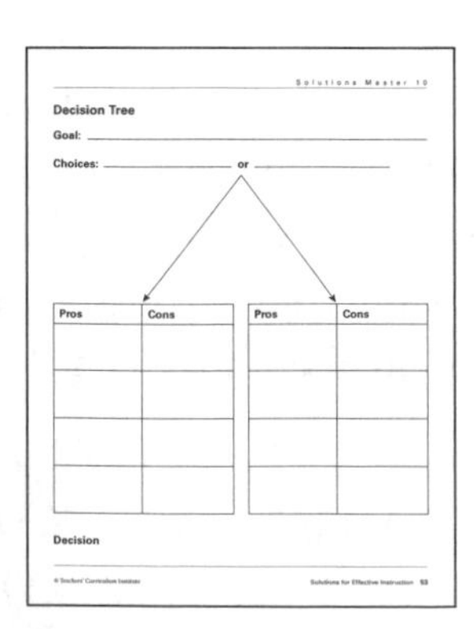
Decision Tree

Goal:

Choices: ____ or ____

Pros	Cons

Pros	Cons

Decision

Solutions Master 10: Decision Tree

Project *Solutions Master 10: Decision Tree.* Suggest a familiar kind of decision to students, such as receiving money for their birthday and having to decide how to spend it. Point to the top of the transparency and tell students that the first thing they should do is identify their goal. For example, they may want to spend the money on a need rather than a want. Or they might just want to make the best choice or get the best value. Record the goal, such as spending money on a want rather than a need, such as an extra or a new baseball cap. List these choices at the top of the decision tree. Next, have students evaluate each choice by thinking about the possible results of each choice or by listing the pros and cons of, or reasons for and against, each choice. For example, one cap may be more popular than the other. The other cap may be cheaper, and leave some money left over for buying something else. One cap may be available at a nearby store, while the other is only online and has extra shipping costs or takes longer to get. When the list of pros and cons is complete, review it with students. Finally, after careful consideration and perhaps, also, discussion, have students make a choice. Record their choice, or decision.

Explain that a decision tree can sometimes have many branches. For example, students might want to decide between three choices of what to do for a science or other project. Note that students can always add branches to a decision tree or create their own decisions trees with many branches.

Practice the Skill Distribute copies of *Solutions Master 10: Decision Tree* to students. Ask students to work alone or in pairs to make a decision about another need or want, or about an environmental choice, such as reusing plastic lunch containers or using the back of sheets of paper. Invite volunteers to share their choices, their evaluations, and their decisions.

Solve Problems

Solving problems involves both analysis and evaluation. Students must break the problem down, first by naming it and then by offering possible solutions. Then they must evaluate the solutions to determine which is best.

Teach the Skill Ask students to name a problem that needs to be solved in your school or in your community. For example, they might say that there is too much traffic near school or on Main Street. Tell students they have just completed the first step in solving problems, which is naming the problem. Ask students to tell what the leaders in their community might do to solve the problem. Lead students to the idea that they must come up with several possible solutions, such as widening the road to make more lanes, running more buses, or putting in bike lanes as well as safe, dry places to park bikes.

Project *Solutions Master 11: Flowchart.* Write the steps in the problem-solving process so far in the first two boxes on the transparency: *1) Name the problem. 2) Come up with possible solutions.* Record the problem and the suggested solutions. Then ask students to say how they feel about each of the solutions to the traffic problem. Some, for example, may say that it is too expensive or difficult to widen the road or that it changes Main Street too much or in bad ways. When students give an opinion on one of the possible solutions, tell them that they are evaluating, or making a judgment about, the possible solution. Record this as step three

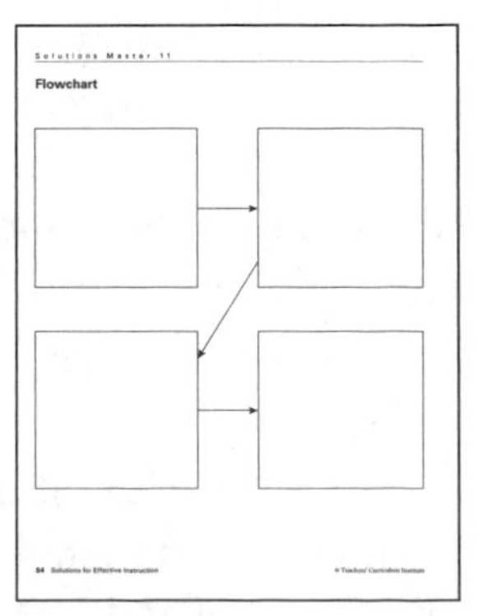

Solutions Master 11: Flowchart

in the process of solving problems: *3) Evaluate the possible solutions.* Explain that problem solvers must look closely at all the possible solutions to determine what they think is good or bad about them. After careful evaluation, the last step in the problem-solving process takes place: *4) Choose a solution.* Label the last box. Review how you would complete the chart using the sample problem you just explored.

Practice the Skill Distribute copies of *Solutions Master 11: Flowchart* to students. Work with students to write labels stating each of the steps in the problem-solving process above the four boxes. Then present a problem that is suggested by the topic you are currently teaching or reviewing. For example, students might look at the problem of pollution through the lens of their own town, neighborhood, school, or home. Suggest pairs of students narrow the concept of pollution to one type of pollution problem and then go through the problem-solving process to suggest the best solution that they, as individuals and schoolchildren, could actually carry out. Leave the completed example on *Solutions Master 11: Flowchart* on display as students work through the process. Review students' completed flowcharts and solutions.

Identify Point of View

Identifying point of view helps students understand how others see things. Determining how a person in a particular place or time saw or experienced events, as well as how people today might have different ideas about an issue because of their different backgrounds, beliefs, jobs, or other factors, helps students develop a richer, fuller sense of the topics they study.

Teach the Skill Put students in groups of four and assign each one a different role based on content you are now teaching or reviewing. For example, to teach or review regions, you might assign these roles: someone who lives in a home on a cattle ranch; someone who lives in a skyscraper in New York; someone who lives in a fishing boat off the Gulf Coast; and someone who lives in a mobile home in the desert. Tell students that each person should feel proud of the place where he or she lives. Then have a group role-play a discussion about the best place to live and why. Ask each student in the group to present ideas from his or her own point of view: that is, based on his or her own experiences, knowledge, and feelings. (For this role-play, students can assume that people playing each role have never been to or lived in the other places or types of homes.) When students are finished, have them talk about how each point of view was limited; that is, how each person knew facts and details only about, or mainly about, his or her own place and type of home. Also discuss what was positive about the different points of view, including how each person was a kind of expert for his or her own region and experience.

Practice the Skill When you introduce, teach, or review a topic that centers on human interactions, such as families and family members, you can deepen the discussion of content and concepts by asking students to think about each person's own or unique point of view. For example, how would a mother or father's point of view about needs or wants be different from a child's point of view?

Analyze Primary and Secondary Sources

An important part of the study of history is distinguishing between the sources we rely on to tell us what happened. When students make distinctions between sources, they begin to understand that some historical accounts are closer to or farther away from the truth than others are. They also begin to understand that people must often use many sources, from both close up and far away, to get a more balanced and complete view of what happened.

Teach the Skill Ask students how they learn about history. Develop a list on the board based on students' replies, such as textbook writing, pictures, stories that older adults tell, museums, and so on. Then talk about how these sources are different by asking students to compare and contrast one primary and secondary source. Project *Solutions Master 1: Venn Diagram* and use it to compare and contrast two sources such as the information in a textbook about an event and a story they learned from an older adult who was at the event. Lead up to a definition of a primary source as a "you are there" or eyewitness account and a secondary source as writing or other information created by people who did not live through the event or time period.

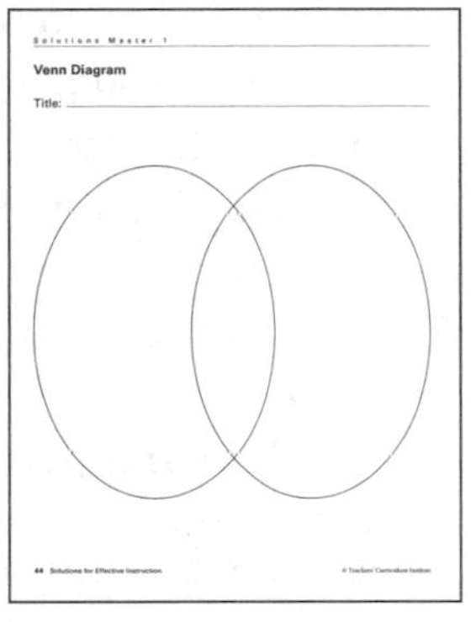

Solutions Master 1: Venn Diagram

Next, project *Solutions Master 2: Two-Column Chart*, and label the headings, *Primary Sources* and *Secondary Sources*. Write and say this list of sources: *diary, newspaper story, photographs, autobiography, biography,* and *textbook writing.* Talk about who would have written each source and when it would have been written. Then ask students to decide which source goes in which column. Record students' answers, being sure to qualify some of the sources by noting, for example, that biographies can go in both columns, depending on when they were written.

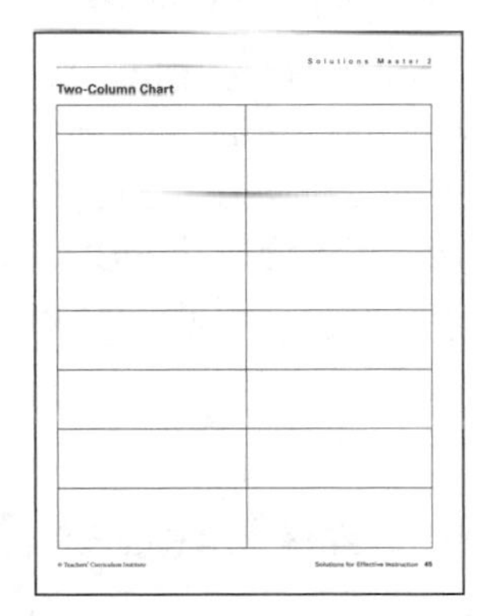

Solutions Master 2: Two-Column Chart

Practice the Skill Give students a primary source on a topic you are studying or have studied as a class, such as the photograph of George Washington Carver teaching his students (Grade 2, page 61), as well as a secondary source on the same topic, which could be the textbook writing or another account. Divide the class into small groups and have them come up with one or more reasons why a primary source could be a good source of information and also why a secondary source could be a good source of information. Then ask them to come up with one way in which each type of source is limited, or lacks something that the other has. Also, ask them to think about how the sources work together to give a more complete picture than just one source alone could give. Have each group present its ideas, and use them to discuss the differences between and uses of primary and secondary sources.

Graphic and Visual Skills: Read Graphs

A graph is a visual way to show numbers of things. The skill of reading graphs teaches students to understand information that is presented visually instead of with text.

Teach the Skill Ask students what they already know about graphs. Elicit or cover these facts as appropriate for your grade: Some graphs are circles with parts that show different things. They are called pie charts. A pie chart uses labels or a key to tell what the parts show. Some graphs use bars to show numbers of things. They are bar graphs. Labels on a bar graph tell what the bars show. Picture graphs use pictures to show numbers of things. A key on the graph usually tells what each picture stands for.

Have students turn to a graph in their textbooks (such as Grade 2, page 92), or have them focus on a classroom graph. Explain or review that no matter what type of graph students are looking at, they should always begin by reading the title or other headings; point out that the title and/or headings help sum up what the graph shows. Their next step is to study the key, if there is one, so that they will know what each picture, symbol, or color on the graph stands for. Explain that not all graphs have a key, however, and sometimes students' next step will be to read other labels on the graph. Then they can focus on what each bar, section, row, or column shows, and how it is different from other information on the graph. Finally, students should summarize what the graph shows. They may do this silently, orally with a partner, or in writing. A summary should begin with the title of the graph, a paraphrase of the title, or a statement identifying the main idea that the graph shows.

Practice the Skill Have students study a different graph (such as one in their math textbook or workbook). With a small group, have them follow these steps: *1) Read the title. 2) Study the key. 3) Read the labels. 4) Read each part, row, column, or bar of the graph and compare it with the other parts, rows, columns, or bars. 5) Summarize.* Call for volunteers from different groups to report their summaries.

Graphic and Visual Skills: Read Flowcharts

The skill of reading flowcharts helps students to understand steps in a process. Using flowcharts can help students develop analytical skills as they break down processes or events into their parts.

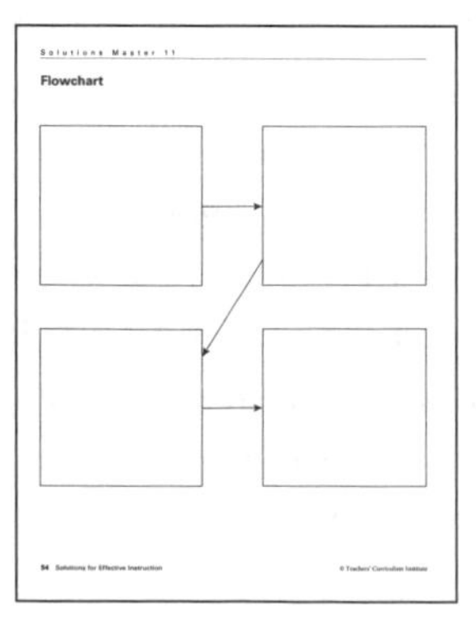

Solutions Master 11: Flowchart

Teach the Skill Project *Solutions Master 11: Flowchart* to reacquaint students with the look of a flowchart, and explain that students should begin reading a flowchart by focusing on the box that is closest to the top, farthest to the left, or both. Then they should follow the directions of the arrows to read separate steps in a process in the order in which they should be performed or events in a sequence of events in the order in which they occurred. Point to the top box and move your finger in the direction of the arrows. Note that a flowchart can have more or fewer than four boxes, and that it may be illustrated. Then name a process related to our environment, such as using trees to meet our needs. Work with students to break it down into steps, such as 1) cutting down the trees, 2) moving the trees to a sawmill, 3) making the trees into boards, 4) making the boards into furniture or houses. Record these steps on the transparency, and review what the completed organizer shows.

Practice the Skill Have students focus on a flowchart displayed in your classroom or a flowchart in one of their textbooks (such as Grade 2, page 75). Ask them to identify what the flowchart shows by reading or paraphrasing the title of the flowchart or the title of the section of the book it comes from. Then have them identify the separate steps in the process.

Graphic and Visual Skills: Use Web Diagrams

Web diagrams, which are also called concept maps, cluster diagrams, and wheel-and-spoke diagrams, help students organize or arrange details around a central opinion, focus, topic, or main idea. Using web diagrams provides excellent practice in analysis. Webs can be used to identify or generate an opinion and reasons, a main idea and details, or a class and its members. In all of these ways, using a web helps students see how ideas relate to one another and to a larger concept. Students can make their own webs to develop, demonstrate, or communicate their understanding of a topic. The skill is applicable to all areas of social studies.

Teach the Skill Project *Solutions Master 5: Web.* Model using a web diagram to organize information. Write the name of a holiday such as Thanksgiving in the center. Ask your students about what they do, what they eat, and why they celebrate the holiday. Use the secondary circles to record ideas such as actions, foods, and meaning. Then draw more circles to give examples of the special foods, activities, or meaning. When the web is completed, have a volunteer summarize what it shows. Talk about why a web diagram can be a good way to show what students have learned.

Solutions Master 5: Web

Practice the Skill Group students in pairs, distribute copies of *Solutions Master 5: Web* to each pair, or ask students to draw their own webs. Have them use their web to show what they have learned about a recent topic under study, such as ways to help at school or groups we belong to. Discuss the completed webs. If you wish, extend teaching to review the skill of analysis, which students have just used to create the web; to review classification; or to teach writing paragraphs that explain by using the center of the web as a basis of a topic sentence and the surrounding circles as the basis of supporting information.

Graphic and Visual Skills: Analyze Timelines

The ability to analyze a timeline is crucial to the study of history. Timelines enable students to view eras and trends as a series of chronological events. Like charts, timelines summarize and simplify information. They provide a kind of brief, chronological outline rather than an in-depth discussion.

Teach the Skill Present a timeline to your students (such as the timeline in Grade 2, pages 112–113), or construct a simple timeline using *Solutions Master 12: Timeline.* Ask students to tell what the timeline shows, reminding them, as needed, always to begin analyzing any chart, table, graph, or other organizer by reading the title and getting an overview in that way. If there is a caption, this may also aid them in the process of summing up what the timeline shows; however, captions sometimes add new information or comment on specific details in the timeline. Explain that the next step in the process of analyzing a timeline is to determine the time span it shows, if this information is not already given in the title. For example, a timeline may show the years 1800–1900 or just one day. After determining the topic and the time span, students should also look at the intervals, that is, the length of time between the marks that show dates on the timeline. This helps them develop a sense of how slowly or rapidly events occurred over time. Next, students should read the individual dates and labels, as well as study any illustrations if they are present. A final step in analyzing timelines is to sum up—orally, silently, or in writing—what the timeline shows.

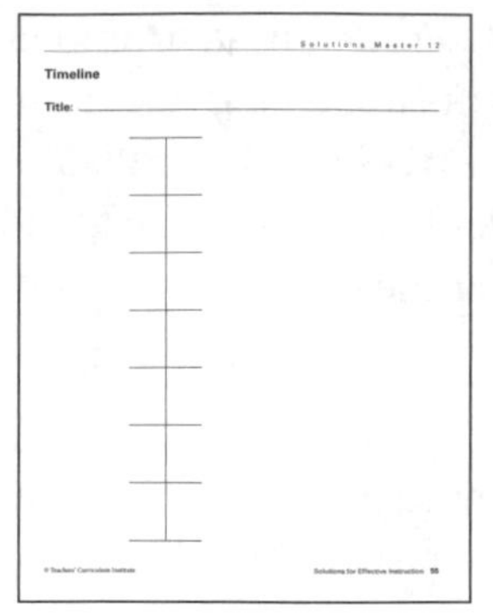

Solutions Master 12: Timeline

Practice the Skill Distribute *Solutions Master 12: Timeline* and have pairs of students use it to make a timeline of their school day yesterday or of a community day, such as Earth Day. As needed, post the events of the day on the board, and suggest intervals for the timeline, such as 9AM, 10 AM, and so on. Have students record all major events of the day, such as when they had reading, when they went to lunch, when they did math, and so on. Have pairs title their graph, share it with another pair, and sum up what it shows.

Graphic and Visual Skills: Analyze Photographs and Other Images

Students can learn about history by analyzing photographs, illustrations, and other images. Sometimes, visual information can express ideas or emotions that the text alone does not convey. Sometimes, visual information also adds to what the text says or presents a slightly different angle on it.

Teach the Skill Display a photo or two from the text that shows something you are teaching or reviewing now, such as the pictures of an old schoolhouse and school room (Grade 1, page 67). Ask, *What is going on in the picture?* Encourage your students to give as much detail as possible, as well as to decide what seems most important in the picture and what seems less or least important. Note that, occasionally, a visual will have a title; usually, it will have a caption. Ask students to identify these elements, if present, and explain what they tell. Discuss how the photo or photos tell some of the same things that the textbook writing tells. Discuss how the photos or photos give new information, too. Remind students always to relate what they see in a photograph or illustration to what they are reading and learning about a topic. Write and read these steps in analyzing a photo or other visual: *1) Study the photo. Look at all the details. 2) Decide what is most important. Decide what is not as important, too. 3) Make connections* *between the photo and what you are learning. Does it repeat what the text says? If so, how? What new information does it give?*

Practice the Skill Have pairs of students select a photograph from a chapter of the textbook that they have recently studied and use the process above to analyze it. Have pairs share their photograph and analysis with other pairs. When both pairs agree about what each photograph shows, have them present their analysies to the class.

Part Two
Integrating Language Arts

Prereading Strategies

Identify Structural Features of Informational Materials

1 Have students point out the different parts of their chapter:

Beginning

- chapter number
- chapter title (Note that it is printed in a different color and different size type; it is not a sentence; and it contains many capital letters.)
- social studies vocabulary
- pictures
- words (text)
- page numbers

Middle

- numbers before headings
- section headings (Note that they are printed in a different color and different size type; they are not sentences; and they contain many capital letters.)
- social studies vocabulary (in text)
- pictures
- words (text)
- summary in a box (grades 1 and 2)
- page numbers

End

- Reading Further heading
- chapter number
- title (Note that it is printed in a different color and different size type; it is not a sentence; and it contains many capital letters.)
- lead-in or intro sentence in heavy black type
- pictures
- words (text)
- page numbers

2 At kindergarten level or as needed, also review the front cover, the back cover, the title page, and reading print from left to right and top to bottom.

3 Hand out *Solutions Master 13: My Social Studies Chapter.* Have students work in pairs to list as many features as they can in each column. Alternatively, project *Solutions Master 13: My Social Studies Chapter,* and work as a class to complete it.

Variation Have each student represent a chapter part. Designate the four corners of your room as "beginning," "middle," "end," or "more than one part of a chapter." Have students go to the correct spot. Have students in the "beginning," "middle," and "end" corners put themselves in order. Have students in the "more than one part of a chapter" corner tell more than one place where their chapter parts go.

Beginning	Middle	End

Solutions Master 13: My Social Studies Chapter

Apply Learning About Structural Features

Photocopy one part of a chapter: beginning, middle, or end. Cut it into parts. Have students work in pairs to put the parts back together in correct order.

Optional Extension Have students glue the parts in order onto sheets of paper. Ask them to say the name of or label each part.

Predict

Have students preview the chapter by reading the headings and looking at the pictures. Have them predict what they will learn.

Optional Extension Have students revise and confirm predictions during and after reading.

Use a KWL Chart

Have students preview the chapter. Hand out *Solutions Master 14: KWL Chart,* and have students complete the first two columns. Alternatively, project the chart as a transparency and complete the first two columns as a class.

KWL Chart

I already know . . .	I want to learn . . .	I learned . . .

Solutions Master 14: KWL Chart

Create an Anticipation Guide

Prepare two or three statements based on chapter content. Write them on the board or hand them out, and read them aloud.

Example *People do activities at home and at school.*

Ask students to agree or disagree with each statement, or ask students to say true or false. Restate and/or record the class consensus.

Model the Guiding Questions Strategy

Turn the first subhead title into a question. Ask students to read to find the answer. Encourage students to continue to use this strategy as they read.

During Reading Strategies

Model the "Talk Back" Strategy

Tell students that it's a great idea to talk back—aloud, if they are alone, or silently—when they read. To model this strategy, read the first section of the chapter and then produce a short summary that begins, *This section tells me that . . .* or *I learned that . . .* Group students in pairs and ask them to continue using this strategy as they read.

Variations Students can also question, react to interesting information, or tell what confuses them.

Provide Tips for Note Taking

1 Photocopy one section of the chapter and project it as a transparency.

2 Read the section aloud as students follow along. Ask them to react by telling you what's important, what's new, or what is hard to understand. Or ask them to tell you what they can see in their mind's eye as they read the text.

3 Model methods of taking notes based on students' answers.

- **Use sticky notes.** Show how you might write * on a sticky note to place next to a main idea, *!* on a sticky to place next to something surprising, or *?* on a sticky note to place next to something confusing.
- **Use graphic organizers.** Show how you might sketch your own main idea and details chart, main idea and details web, or other organizer to record information.
- **Sketch.** Show how you might make simple sketches or diagrams as you read.

Make Connections Chart

In my book . . .	In my life . . .

Solutions Master 15: Make Connections Chart

Use the Make Connections Chart

Distribute copies of *Solutions Master 15: Make Connections Chart* or project it as a transparency. Help students list chapter content and make connections to their own life. For example, students might link the concepts of a school custodian and principal to the actual people who play those roles, such as Mr. Samperi or Ms. Jefferson, in their own school.

Reinforce Sequencing Skills

For chapters that are organized by chronological order or that include steps in a process, have students identify what happens first (or what to do first), next, and so on. Distribute copies of *Solutions Master 3: Sequence Chain* and have students work in pairs to record chronological order or steps in a process. Depending on chapter content, explain that students may need to add more boxes.

Variation When a chapter lists many events or steps in a process, it might be possible for small groups of students to form a human flowchart, sequence chain, or timeline. Each student, pair, or small group of students should hold a sheet of paper with one event or step written clearly in big letters and line up in order.

Solutions Master 3: Sequence Chain

Analyze Cause and Effect

For chapters that include a single cause and effect, a single cause and multiple effects, or a single effect with multiple causes, display *Solutions Master 4: Cause-and-Effect Diagram* and model how you would complete the first box, as well as how you might not use all the boxes or add some boxes. Then distribute copies of *Solutions Master 4: Cause-and-Effect Diagram* for students to complete.

Use a Diagram to Compare and Contrast

For chapters that include both significant comparisons and important contrasts, distribute copies of *Solutions Master 1: Venn Diagram*, or project it as a transparency. Work as a class to create a title for the Venn diagram. Review what to write in each part of the diagram. Have students complete the diagram individually or in pairs.

Use Charts to Compare or Contrast

For chapters that present comparisons or contrasts, distribute copies of either *Solutions Master 2: Two-Column Chart* or *Solutions Master 16: Three-Column Chart*, or project it as a transparency. Work as a class to create a title for the chart and the column headings. Then complete the chart as a class, or have students complete the chart individually or in pairs.

Identify Narrative Information

For chapters that retell events, distribute copies of *Solutions Master 17: 5W Chart*, or project it as a transparency. Work as a class to create a title for the chart. Have students complete the chart individually or in pairs.

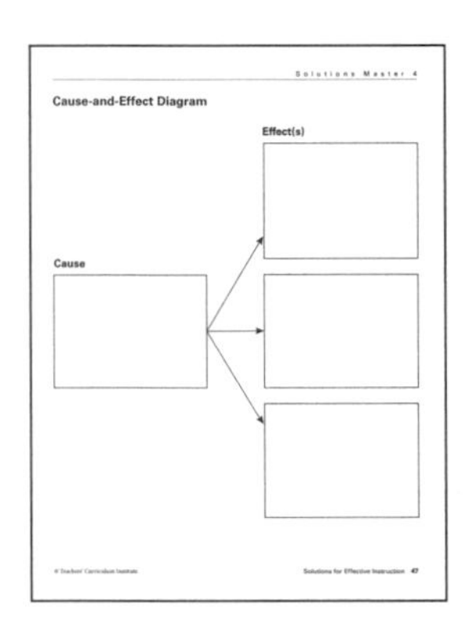

Solutions Master 4:
Cause-and-Effect Diagram

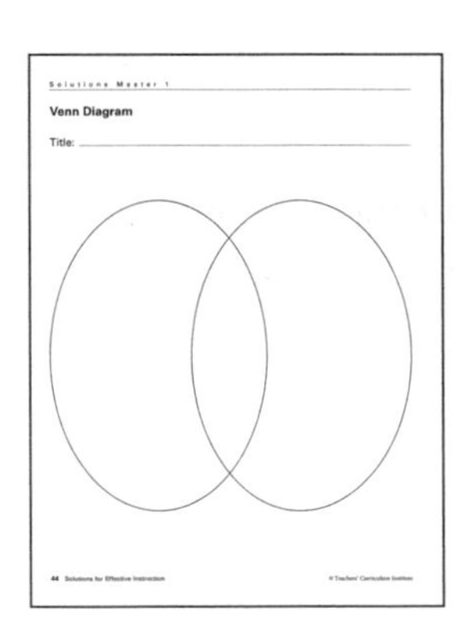

Solutions Master 1:
Venn Diagram

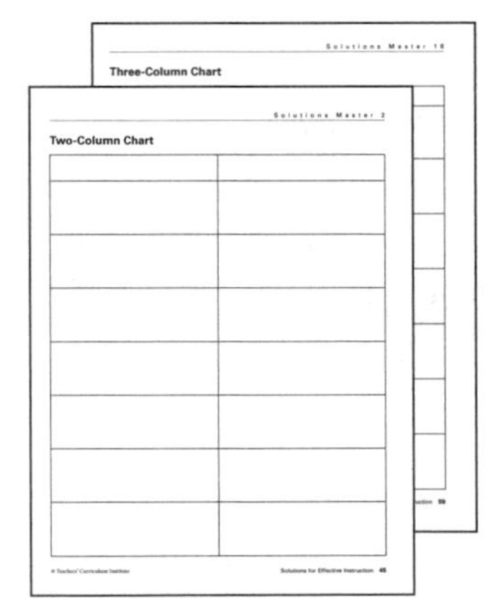

Solutions Master 2:
Two-Column Chart
Solutions Master 16:
Three-Column Chart

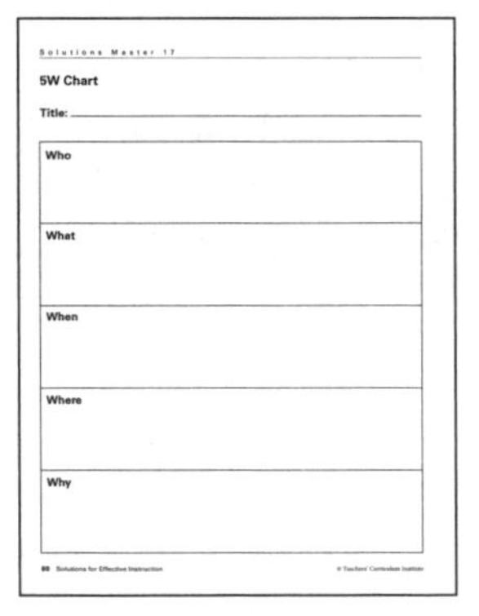

Solutions Master 17:
5W Chart

Create a Web of the Main Idea and Supporting Details

Project or distribute *Solutions Master 5: Web.* Explain that, usually, a chapter section presents one main idea. Help students identify the main idea of a section and record it in the center of the web. Then have students identify the details that tell about or explain the main idea and record them in the secondary circles.

Variation Use the transparency with individual paragraphs or with the chapter as a whole.

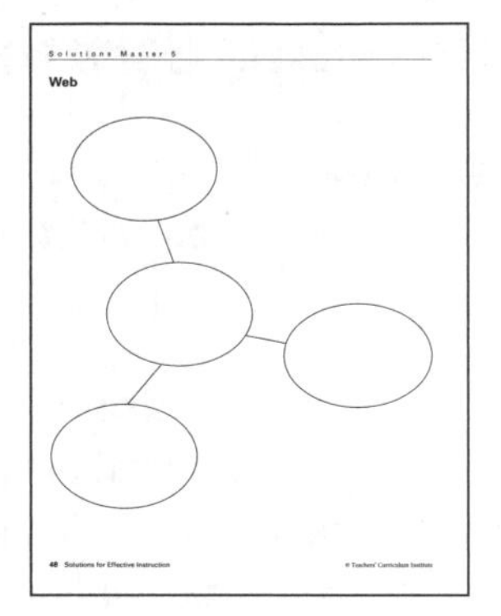

Solutions Master 5: Web

Create a Chart of the Main Idea and Details

Project *Solutions Master 9: Support Chart.* Explain that, usually, a chapter section presents one main idea. Help students identify the main idea of a section and record it in the top box of the transparency. Then have students identify the details that tell about or explain the main idea and record them in the remaining boxes of the chart.

Variations

- Use the transparency as a basis for teaching summarizing. Have students identify what belongs in a summary and what doesn't.
- Use the transparency with individual paragraphs or with the chapter as a whole.

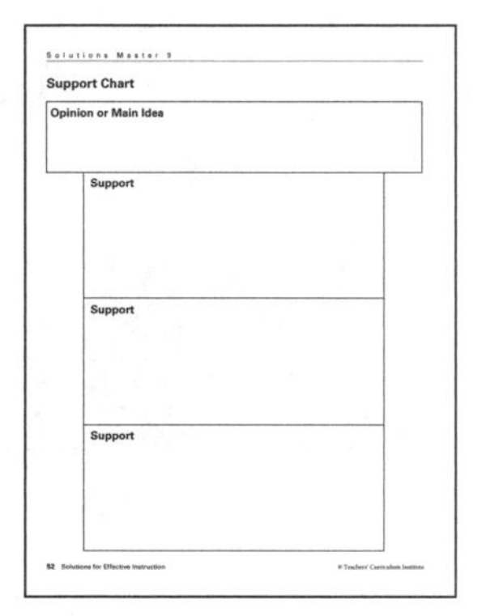

Solutions Master 9: Support Chart

Apply Learning About the Main Idea and Details

Photocopy one section of a chapter. Cut it into parts that include the main idea and details or other explanation. Have students work in pairs to identify the parts and to put the parts back together in correct order.

Optional Extension Have students glue the parts in order onto sheets of paper. Ask them to say the name of or label each part as the main idea or details.

Acknowledge and Categorize Learning

Help students identify main ideas by contributing to a class chart. First, create a poster or chart titled *What I Learned Today About . . .* Have each student write a response on a sticky note and put it on the class chart. Review the results as a class. Remove duplicates. Then challenge students to sort notes into main ideas and details.

After Reading Strategies

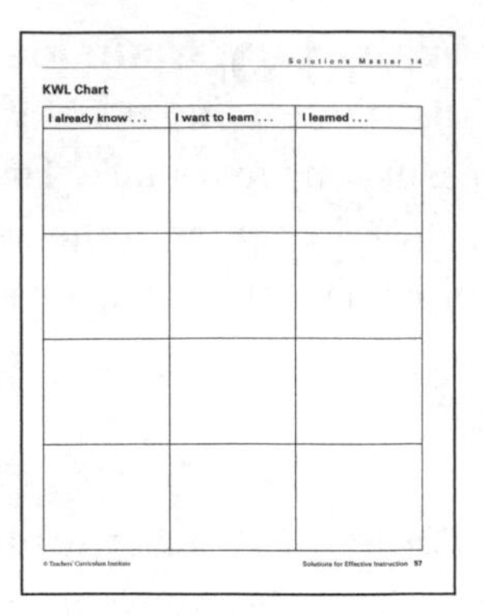
KWL Chart

I already know . . .	I want to learn . . .	I learned . . .

Solutions Master 14: KWL Chart

Use a KWL Chart

Return to the *Solutions Master 14: KWL Chart*, and have students complete the last column.

Return to the Anticipation Guide

If there is a strong pedagogical purpose for doing so, such as a common misconception about chapter content that surfaced during prereading, return to and discuss the statements that students responded to before reading the chapter.

Find Answers in the Text

Pose recall questions and have students point to or use a sticky note to identify the exact place in the text where the answers are found.

Sum It Up

Have students use section heads to sum up the content of each section.

Return to Reading Graphic Organizers

Have students use any graphic organizers they filled in during reading to summarize chapter or section content or to identify gaps in their knowledge, problems, or questions.

Summarize 3-2-1

Have students summarize by stating the following:

- 3 new things they found out
- 2 interesting things they learned
- 1 question they still have

Create a Hand Summary

Have students trace the outline of their hand on a piece of paper. Tell them to write the subject or main idea inside the outline of the thumb. Have them use the fingers to list details that help tell about the topic.

Create Exit Slips

Have students write an "Exit Slip" by having them freewrite for five minutes on what they learned from the chapter. Students do not need to worry about order or organization in this exercise but should instead strive to record all the main ideas and details they can recall.

Reflect

Have students reflect on the following:

- things they learned
- ways they learned
- strategies they can use to learn when they study the next chapter

Vocabulary Development Strategies

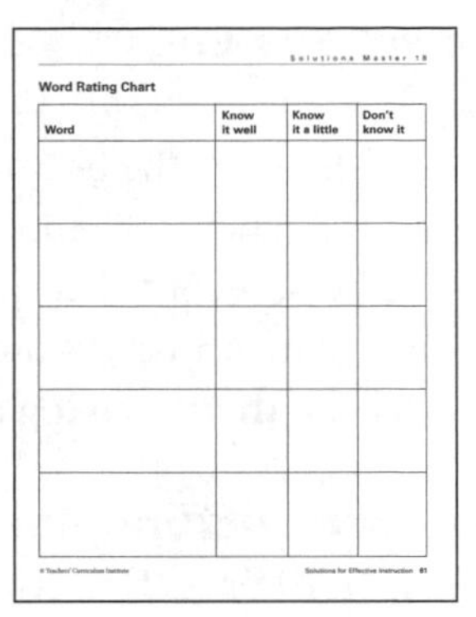

Word Rating Chart

Word	Know it well	Know it a little	Don't know it

Solutions Master 18: Word Rating Chart

Use a Word Rating Chart

Point out the chapter vocabulary and say each word aloud. Distribute *Solutions Master 18: Word Rating Chart*, and have students cross out or add boxes so that they have the same number as the number of new terms in the chapter. Have students complete the rating chart on their own.

Use Syllabication in the Decoding Process

Write chapter social studies words of two or more syllables. Draw lines between the syllables. Point to the letters that represent the sounds as you slowly say each syllable. Then say the words slowly again and have students clap out the syllables.

Variation Emphasize blending the phonemes that make up the syllables.

Decode with Vowel and Consonant Patterns

Write the social studies words. Model decoding them. Note *CVC, CVVC, VCCV, VCV, VCe,* open and closed syllables, and other vowel and consonant patterns.

Decode with Common Syllable Patterns

Write the social studies words. Model decoding them. Note open syllables, closed syllables, *VCe* syllables, vowel-*r* syllables, vowel pair syllables, and final stable syllables.

Decode and Analyze Multisyllable Words

For social studies words with three syllables, draw or distribute parts or an outline of a three-part word bug or word train. Have students record the syllables at the beginning, middle, and end of the word and then join the word parts in order with tape or glue.

Optional Extensions

- Display completed word bugs or word trains. Have pairs of students read them to each other.
- Have students use the word bugs or word trains as flashcards and create clues and riddles for them.

Identify Affixes and Roots

Write the social studies words. Have students identify familiar prefixes, suffixes, base words, or roots. Have them name other words that share the same word part.

Example ***reuse****—redo, remake, rewrite; useful, useless, used*

Variation Write the social studies word but leave blanks for key word parts, such as a prefix, base, root, or suffix. Have students supply the word part.

Keep a Word Parts Log

Project *Solutions Master 19: My Word Parts Log.* Show how you would record a word such as *feelings* in the bottom part of the log because it has the familiar suffixes *-ing* and *-s*. Then ask students for the meaning of the word, relate it to the familiar suffixes, record the meaning, and talk about how the familiar word parts help you understand the word. Distribute copies of the solution master and ask students to keep their own log of familiar word parts.

Solutions Master 19:
My Word Parts Log

Use a Web for Structural Analysis

For words with word parts that students can use to make useful generalizations to other words, project *Solutions Master 5: Web.* Write one social studies word in the center of the web. Have students name other words with the same word part and record them.

Examples ***inventor***—*tutor, author, mentor;* ***leader***—*voter, teacher, writer*

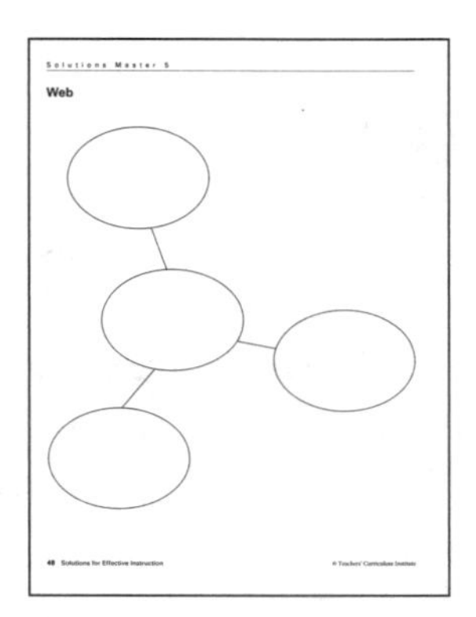

Solutions Master 5:
Web

Develop Word Families

Write each social studies vocabulary word. Have students name words in the same family. List the words.

Example ***play***—*player, playing, played, replay*

Variation Use *Solutions Master 5: Web* to lead the class in this activity or to provide a framework or organizing structure for students to use on their own.

Present Cognates

Help students whose native language is Spanish to make connections by presenting the following cognates as they learn each related social studies word:

Kindergarten *diferente, familia, tradición, solucionar/resolvar, problema, adulto, estado (state), símbolo, reciclar (recycle), reducir*

Grade 1 *diferente, secretario, respetar, mapa, símbolo, dirección, escuela (school), familia, communidad, actividades, mover (to move), tradición, celebración*

Grade 2 *urbano, rural, suburbio, suburbano, símbolo, geografía, montaña, valle, rio, desierto, lago (lake), isla, océano, continente, naturaleza (nature), transporte, canal, servicios, plaza, historia, inventor, votante (voter), gobierno (government), leglislatura, esclavitud (slavery), turista, colonia*

Reinforce Alphabetical Order

Have students write the social studies words in alphabetical order.

Use Initial, Medial, and Final Sounds to Decode

Say two social studies words. Have students decide if they heard the same beginning sound. As applicable, repeat with medial and final sounds.

Use Rhyming Words to Decode

Say a social studies word. Ask students to name a rhyming word.

Change Initial, Medial, and Final Sounds to Decode

Say the social studies words. Then say a familiar word such as *tool*. Ask students which social studies word they would get if they changed the /t/ to /sk/. Review how changing medial and final sounds would yield other familiar words.

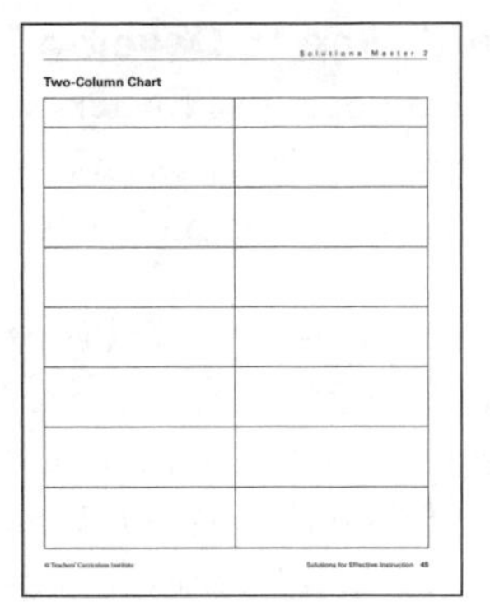

Solutions Master 2: Two-Column Chart

Identify Initial, Medial, and Final Sounds to Decode

Say a social studies word and ask students how many sounds they hear. Encourage students to count on their fingers as they repeat each word slowly to identify all the sounds.

Identify Words in a Spoken Context

Say the social studies words in sentences and ask students to clap or raise their hands when they hear the word.

Identify Shared Initial, Medial, and Final Sounds

Say three social studies words and ask students to identify whether any of the words have any of the same sounds.

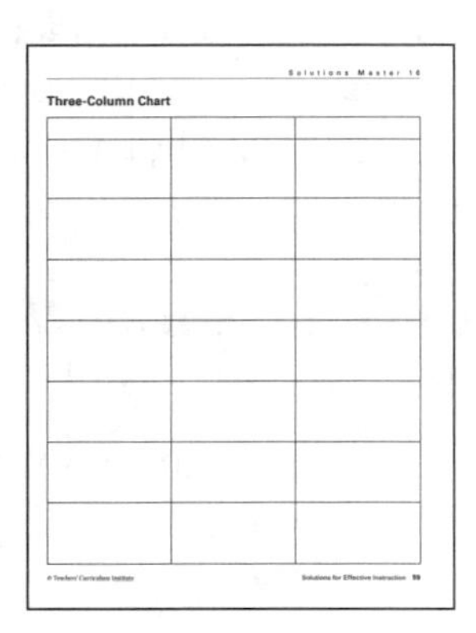

Solutions Master 16: Three-Column Chart

Sort by Structure, Function, or Meaning

Have students sort social studies vocabulary into categories such as the following:

- one-syllable, two-syllable, and three-syllable words
- naming words, action words, describing words
- words and phrases
- words that are compound and not compound
- content categories, such as people and places, or people, places, and things

Hand out, as appropriate, *Solutions Master 2: Two-Column Chart* or *Solutions Master 16: Three-Column Chart*. Have students work in pairs to label the columns and to list words in the correct column. Alternatively, project *Solutions Master 2: Two-Column Chart* or *Solutions Master 16: Three-Column Chart*, and work as a class to complete it.

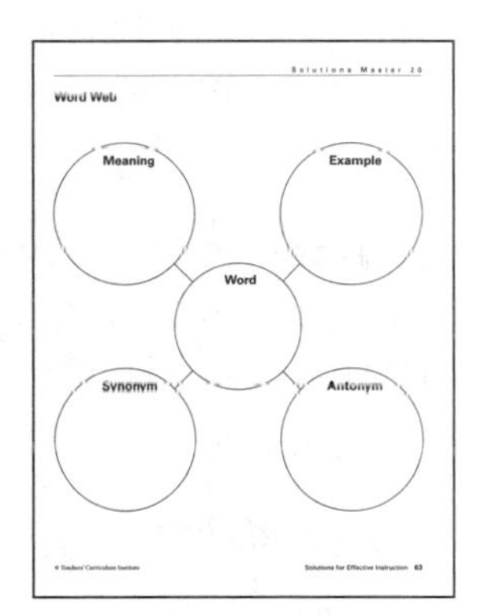

Solutions Master 20: Word Web

Use a Word Web to Develop Meaning

For words that have synonyms and antonyms, as well as words that name categories, project *Solutions Master 20: Word Web*. Model how to complete it with a sample word or a review word. Then distribute copies of the word web, assign a social studies word, and have students work individually or in pairs to complete it.

Use a Word Map to Develop Meaning

For words that appear in the text with clear and easily recognizable context clues, distribute copies of *Solutions Master 21: Word Map.* Have students work individually or in pairs to complete it.

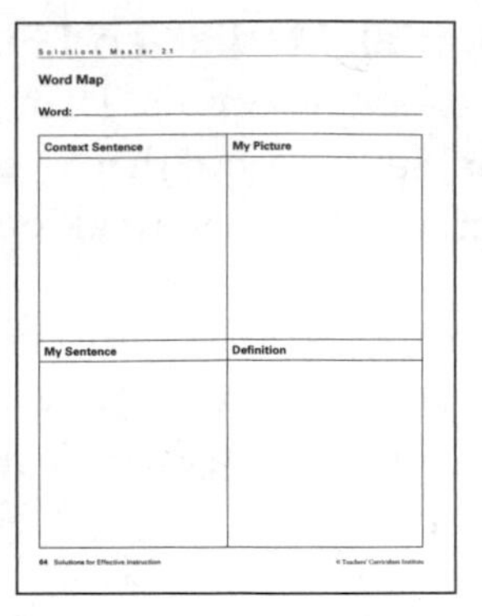

Solutions Master 21: Word Map

Use a Word Wheel to Develop Meaning

Project *Solutions Master 22: Word Wheel.* Write a social studies word with a familiar word part in the middle of the circle. Label the outer segments of the circle *Kind of Word, Familiar Word Part,* and *Related Words.* (Or vary these labels as the words demand; for example, students might record syllables, synonyms, or words and phrases that the target word brings to mind.) Start by having the students identify whether the word is a naming word, action word, or describing word. Write their answer under *Kind of Word.* Then have students identify a familiar word part, such as the prefix *re-* or the suffix *-er* and record it under *Familiar Word Part.* Finally, have students name words with the same word part, and record them under *Related Words.*

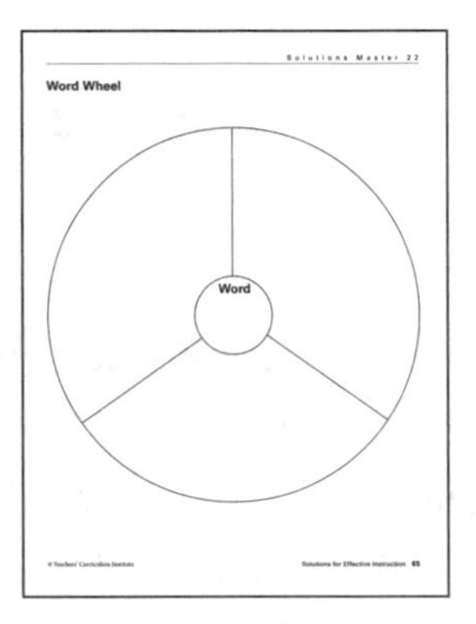

Solutions Master 22: Word Wheel

Use Categories to Develop Meaning

Say and write a vocabulary word. Ask students to name a category it fits into.

Example Say *principal.* Students might answer people, people at school, leaders, three-syllable words, words that begin with *p* or *pr,* and so on.

Variations

- Say and write a vocabulary word, such as *state, goods, activities,* or *suburbs.* Have students name words that belong in the category that the word names.
- Project *Solutions Master 22: Word Wheel.* Write the social studies word in the middle of the Word Wheel. Have students name examples that fit into the category and record them.

Make Connections to the Senses

Say and write a vocabulary word. As applicable, have students complete these sentence starters orally or in writing:

[The word] looks like . . .

[The word] sounds like . . .

[The word] feels like . . .

Map Word Meaning

Distribute copies of *Solutions Master 23: Getting to Know a Word.* Have students write a target social studies word at the top of the page. Guide students to complete the organizer, or have them complete it in pairs or on their own by writing the chapter title, section title, or other description of the context in which they learned the word; listing the other social studies vocabulary words they learned with the new word; speculating on ways to use the word; and coming up with their own method for remembering it.

Solutions Master 23: Getting to Know a Word

Use a Word Wall

Add social studies words to your word wall or create a word wall for them.

Use a Pocket Chart

- Use letters in your pocket chart to create social studies words.
- Add social studies words or word parts to your pocket chart or create a pocket chart for them.

Make Word Ladders

Have students make word ladders. Word ladder options include adding one letter, changing one letter, deleting one letter, and anagramming.

Examples ***want***—*ant, an;* **learn**—*real, are, re*

Make Shorter Words from Longer Words

Have students make as many smaller words as they can from one longer word.

Make Word Crosses

Have students make word crosses with the social studies vocabulary words. Students may use pen and paper, classroom letter cards, or letter cards from a language arts program.

Play 5 Questions

Put students into groups and have each choose a social studies word from the current chapter or a word they have already learned. Then have them play a game of 5 Questions, posing questions such as, *Does it begin with a consonant? Does it have a short* a *sound? Does it name a place?*

Use Riddles

- Have students choose the hardest word and make up a rhyme, riddle, or other mnemonic for recalling it.
- Have students create word riddles by giving the clues one by one, such as, *it begins with a consonant, it has a short a sound, and it names a place,* and have a partner guess the word.

Optional Extension Have students make a book of social studies word riddles.

Play Tic-Tac-Toe

Have students play tic-tac-toe with social studies words and words that follow the same structural or phonemic patterns.

Examples
Kindergarten Player 1 writes *same* in the middle and tries to make tic-tac-toe with other words that begin with the /s/ sound. Player 2 writes *play* and tries to make tic-tac-toe with other words that rhyme with *play.*

Grade 1 Player 1 writes *take turns* in the middle and tries to make tic-tac-toe with phrases, while player 2 writes *listen* and tries to make tic-tac-toe with words with a CVC pattern.

Grade 2 Player 1 writes *lake* in the middle and tries to make tic-tac-toe with words that end in silent *e*. Player 2 writes *transportation* and tries to make tic-tac-toe with words that end in *-tion*.

Present and Use Words in Context

Dictate sentences that use the social studies words. Have students write the sentences. Have students rewrite the sentences as questions.

Variations

- Dictate questions that use the words. Have students change the questions to statements. Or have students answer the questions using complete sentences.
- Dictate commands that use the words. Have students write the commands. Then have them change the commands to statements.

Identify and Use Context Clues

Have students find unfamiliar words in the chapter. Then have students identify context clues and use them to help find the meaning or part of the meaning of the word.

Pair Vocabulary and High-Frequency Words

Write addition operations that include a high-frequency word and a social studies word. Challenge students to write or say a phrase or sentence that uses both words.

Example ***map*** **+** ***has***—The map has different colors.

Pair Social Studies Words and Academic Vocabulary

Write addition operations that include a high-frequency word and an academic vocabulary word. Challenge students to write or say a phrase or sentence that uses both words.

Example ***island*** **+** ***seems***—The island seems small.

Make an Illustrated Dictionary

Have students use sheets of paper, columns on a spreadsheet, separate word processing files, or index cards to make entries for an illustrated dictionary. After several lessons, have students alphabetize their entries and print out their spreadsheet, or put their entries into a word processing document or a booklet called "My Social Studies Dictionary."

Play a Matching Game

Create word cards with social studies vocabulary from several chapters, as well as other familiar words. Have students match words that name people with words that name places; or actions with places; or people with events; or things with places; or things with people.

Examples

Matches for action and place: learn + school; pollute + oceans

Match for person and action: adult + calm down

Match for people and thing or people and event: family + tradition

Generate Context

Use a social studies word to write or say a sentence about a picture in the text.

Variation Have students use a social studies word to write about something in the classroom or in your town or city.

Writing Process Overview Strategies

Present and Use a Writing Process Checklist

For kindergarten, distribute copies of *Solutions Master 24: My Writing Process Checklist*. For grades 1 and 2, distribute copies of either *Solutions Master 25: My Writing Process Checklist for Explaining or Describing* or *Solutions Master 26: My Writing Process Checklist for Stories, Steps, or Events.* Have students tell what the word *process* means in *writing process* or name processes they go through, such as getting ready for school. Explain how everything that students read in their textbook has been through a long writing process. Review stages of the writing process and have students come up with new names for each, or provide terms that students might match with each stage, such as *coming up with ideas, putting ideas on paper, making my writing better,* and *sharing writing.*

Create Writing Process People or Animals Using Describing Words

Assign one stage of the writing process to a pair or small group and have them tell about or describe a kind of person or animal they imagine when they think of the stage. For example, they might imagine prewriting as a busy, excited, or creative person. Prewriting might be wearing red or orange, doing somersaults and back flips, or speeding along in a fast car, while Revising might be a quiet type dressed in black, sitting with his or her head propped up by one hand. Ask students to tell why they came up with the describing words that they did.

Variations

- Have students illustrate the steps in the writing process.
- Have students use their ideas or their drawings to create metaphors for the writing process, such as prewriting is a jet or a cheetah; drafting is a half-built house or a cocoon; publishing is a news program or songbird.
- Have students in Grades 1 and 2 relate stages of the writing process to their social studies vocabulary. For example, at which stage do they *share, introduce, solve problems, follow directions, talk to others, help others, respect others, share what they know,* and *change*?

Set Up a Describing Words Round Robin

Write vocabulary words on cards, such as *family, talk, listen, neighbor, help each other,* and *island*. Distribute several cards to small groups. Have each member of the group add one possible describing word to the card (such as *large, happy; slowly, loudly; carefully, quietly, next-door, nice; every day, at school; small, faraway*), and pass it along to the next person to add another. Continue around the group. Share the describing words as a class. Note how students can add describing words in the same way when they write.

Use Visuals

Remind students that they can add visuals to their writing to help show ideas. Point out examples in your textbook of how charts, graphs, maps, timelines, and other visuals work with the words to give information.

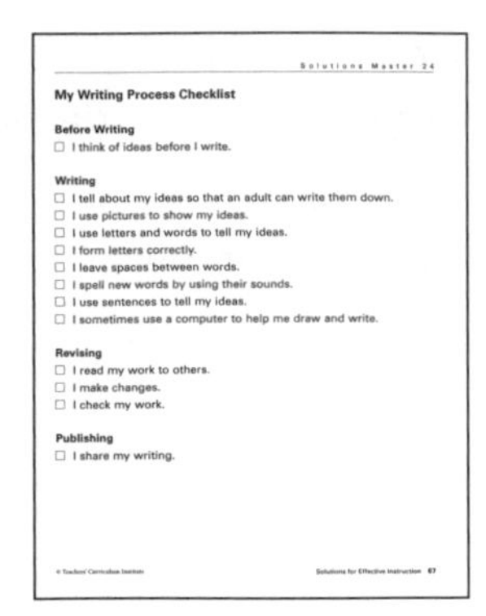

Solutions Master 24

My Writing Process Checklist

Before Writing
- ☐ I think of ideas before I write.

Writing
- ☐ I tell about my ideas so that an adult can write them down.
- ☐ I use pictures to show my ideas.
- ☐ I use letters and words to tell my ideas.
- ☐ I form letters correctly.
- ☐ I leave spaces between words.
- ☐ I spell new words by using their sounds.
- ☐ I use sentences to tell my ideas.
- ☐ I sometimes use a computer to help me draw and write.

Revising
- ☐ I read my work to others.
- ☐ I make changes.
- ☐ I check my work.

Publishing
- ☐ I share my writing.

© Teachers' Curriculum Institute — Solutions for Effective Instruction 67

Solutions Master 24:
My Writing Process Checklist

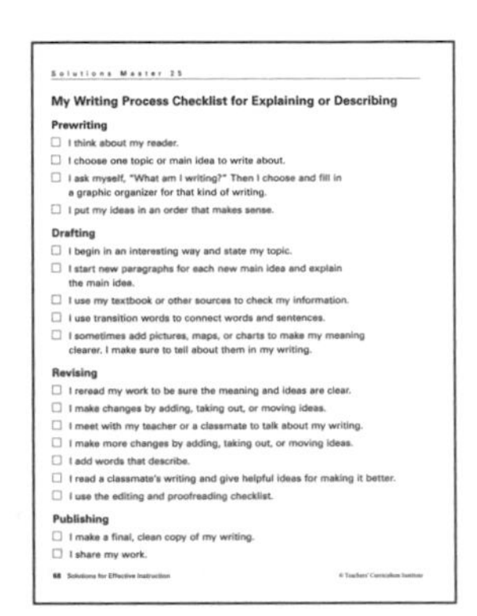

Solutions Master 25

My Writing Process Checklist for Explaining or Describing

Prewriting
- ☐ I think about my reader.
- ☐ I choose one topic or main idea to write about.
- ☐ I ask myself, "What am I writing?" Then I choose and fill in a graphic organizer for that kind of writing.
- ☐ I put my ideas in an order that makes sense.

Drafting
- ☐ I begin in an interesting way and state my topic.
- ☐ I start new paragraphs for each new main idea and explain the main idea.
- ☐ I use my textbook or other sources to check my information.
- ☐ I use transition words to connect words and sentences.
- ☐ I sometimes add pictures, maps, or charts to make my meaning clearer. I make sure to tell about them in my writing.

Revising
- ☐ I reread my work to be sure the meaning and ideas are clear.
- ☐ I make changes by adding, taking out, or moving ideas.
- ☐ I meet with my teacher or a classmate to talk about my writing.
- ☐ I make more changes by adding, taking out, or moving ideas.
- ☐ I add words that describe.
- ☐ I read a classmate's writing and give helpful ideas for making it better.
- ☐ I use the editing and proofreading checklist.

Publishing
- ☐ I make a final, clean copy of my writing.
- ☐ I share my work.

68 Solutions for Effective Instruction — © Teachers' Curriculum Institute

Solutions Master 25:
My Writing Process Checklist
for Explaining or Describing

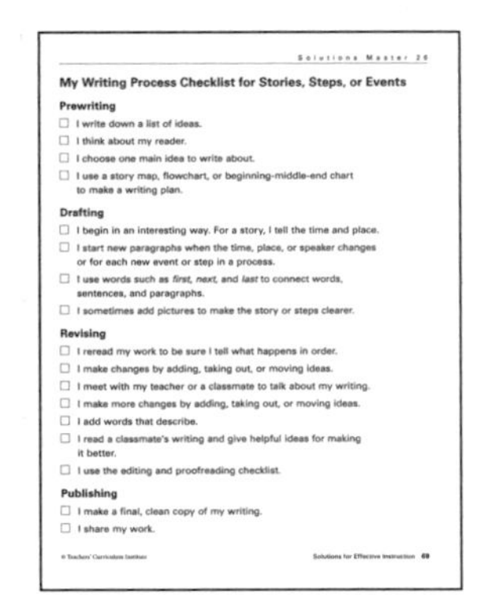

Solutions Master 26

My Writing Process Checklist for Stories, Steps, or Events

Prewriting
- ☐ I write down a list of ideas.
- ☐ I think about my reader.
- ☐ I choose one main idea to write about.
- ☐ I use a story map, flowchart, or beginning-middle-end chart to make a writing plan.

Drafting
- ☐ I begin in an interesting way. For a story, I tell the time and place.
- ☐ I start new paragraphs when the time, place, or speaker changes or for each new event or step in a process.
- ☐ I use words such as *first, next,* and *last* to connect words, sentences, and paragraphs.
- ☐ I sometimes add pictures to make the story or steps clearer.

Revising
- ☐ I reread my work to be sure I tell what happens in order.
- ☐ I make changes by adding, taking out, or moving ideas.
- ☐ I meet with my teacher or a classmate to talk about my writing.
- ☐ I make more changes by adding, taking out, or moving ideas.
- ☐ I add words that describe.
- ☐ I read a classmate's writing and give helpful ideas for making it better.
- ☐ I use the editing and proofreading checklist.

Publishing
- ☐ I make a final, clean copy of my writing.
- ☐ I share my work.

© Teachers' Curriculum Institute — Solutions for Effective Instruction 69

Solutions Master 26:
My Writing Process Checklist
for Stories, Steps, or Events

Use Software and Internet Resources

Encourage students to use appropriate software and the Internet at various stages of the writing process.

Prewriting Students can list, make spreadsheets, and use drawing tools. They may be able to access graphic organizers.

Writing Students can word process; refer to dictionaries, thesauruses, and other tools that are part of their software or on the Internet; find or verify information online; and download free art for their writing, speaking presentations, and illustrated dictionaries.

Revising and Editing Students can use spelling and grammar checks, as long as they do not rely entirely upon them; use editing tools and second colors to highlight and revise; use various software options for graphs, charts, and other visuals; download pictures; create covers; and revise and print out clean final copies.

Prewriting Strategies

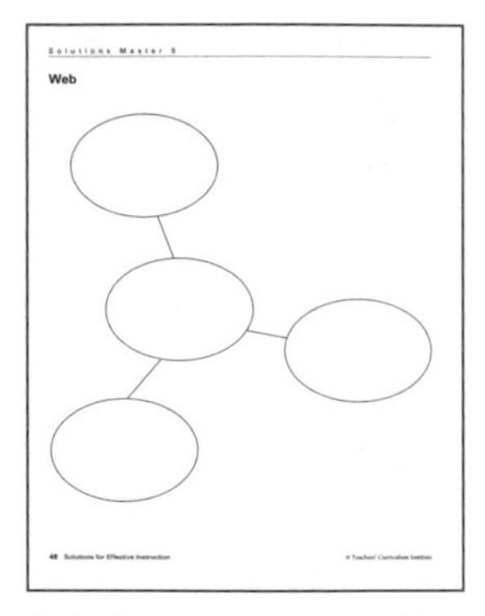

Solutions Master 5: Web

Get Ideas for Expository Writing

When the topic or writing purpose is open, have students brainstorm, list ideas, or freewrite to come up with ideas for writing. Model the process, noting how you select the best idea from your list after you have come up with several ideas.

Get and/or Organize Ideas for Presenting a Main Idea and Details

Hand out copies of *Solutions Master 5: Web.*

- If students are just beginning to prewrite, have them record their topic in the center of the web and other ideas in the outer circles.
- If students are at the organizing stage, have them write their topic in the center and main ideas for paragraphs in the outer circles.

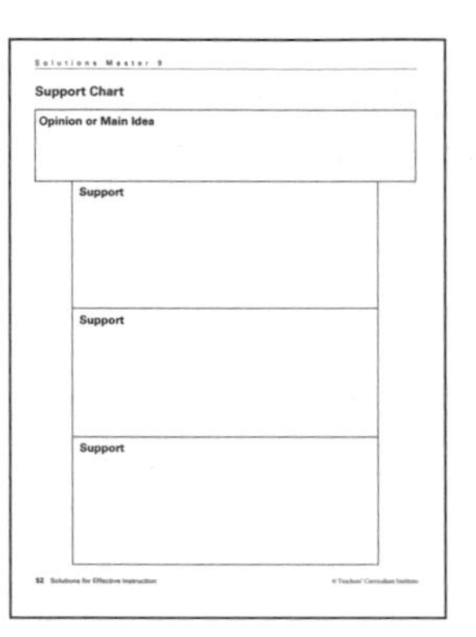

Solutions Master 9: Support Chart

Organize Ideas for Presenting a Main Idea and Details

Hand out copies of *Solutions Master 9: Support Chart.* Have students write their main idea at the top and details that explain or develop their main idea in the spaces marked *Support.*

Get and/or Organize Ideas for Presenting Comparison and Contrast

Hand out copies of *Solutions Master 1: Venn Diagram.* Also display the master as a transparency to model how students should record their topic as a title and label the two outer circles with the names of the things they are comparing and contrasting. Model how to use the outer circles to write things that are different and the overlapping area to write things that are the same.

Get and/or Organize Ideas for Presenting Contrasts

Hand out copies of *Solutions Master 2: Two-Column Chart* or *Solutions Master 16: Three-Column Chart.* Show students how to use each organizer to record their ideas about what they are contrasting.

Get and/or Organize Ideas for Presenting Cause and Effect

Project *Solutions Master 4: Cause-and-Effect Diagram.* Show students how to use the diagram to record one cause with one or more effects or one effect with one or more causes.

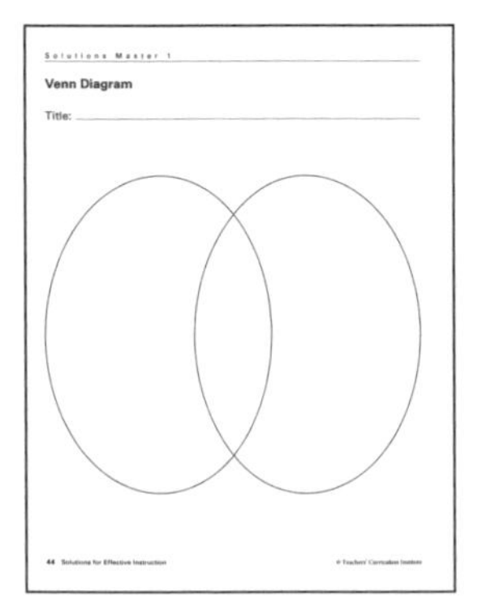

Solutions Master 1: Venn Diagram

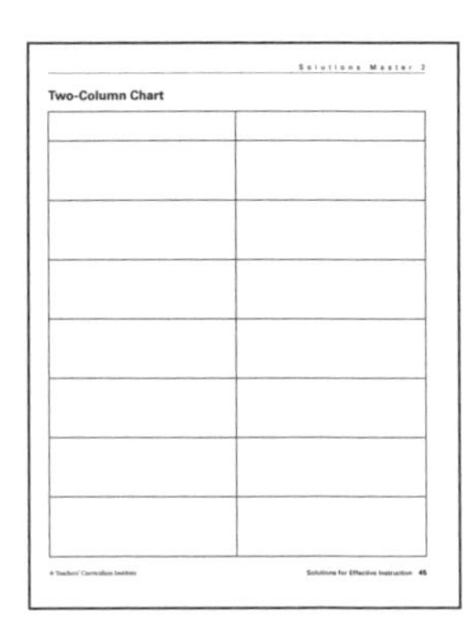

Solutions Master 2: Two-Column Chart

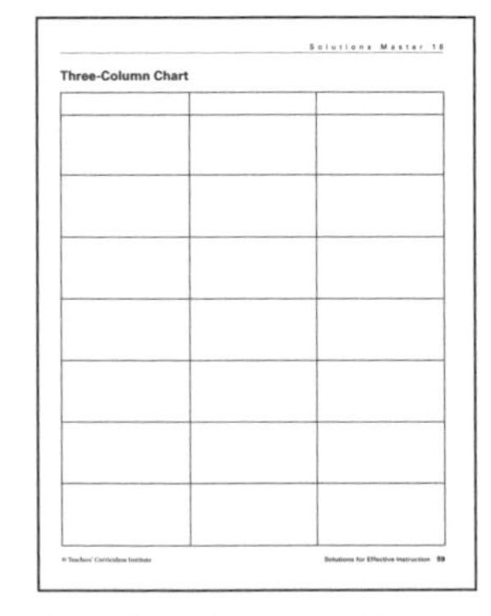

Solutions Master 16: Three-Column Chart

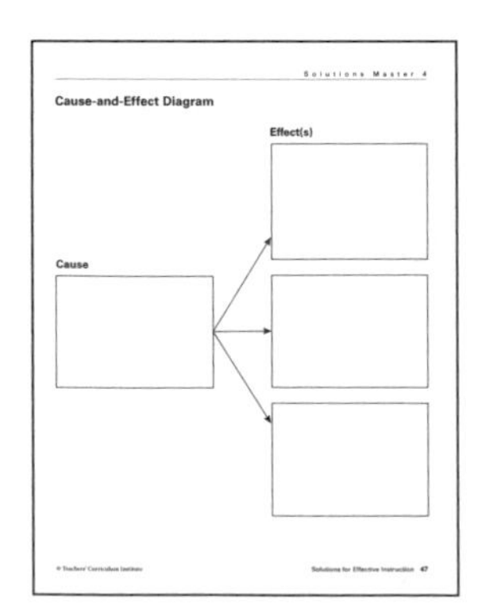

Solutions Master 4: Cause-and-Effect Diagram

Get and/or Organize Ideas for Narrating

Hand out copies of *Solutions Master 3: Sequence Chain.* Have students use each box to record one event or step in a process. Note that students can add extra boxes on the back if they need them.

Variations Hand out copies of *Solutions Master 17: 5W Chart, Solutions Master 27: Story Map,* or *Solutions Master 28: Beginning-Middle-End Chart.* Show students how to use each organizer to jot down narrative ideas or parts.

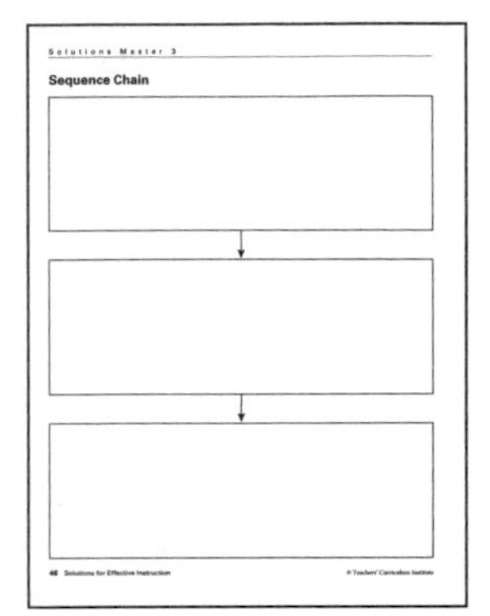
Sequence Chain

Solutions Master 3:
Sequence Chain

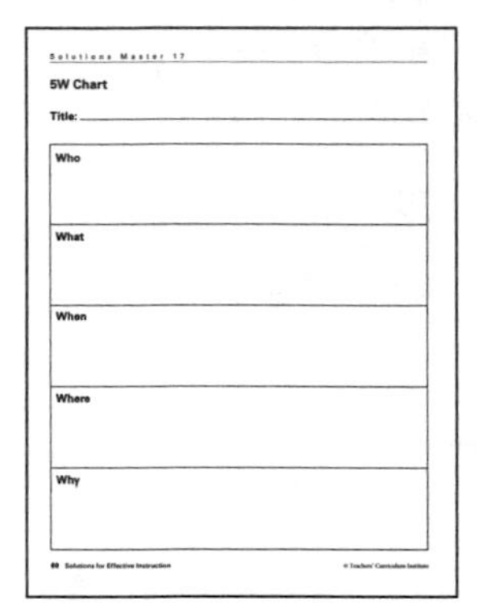
5W Chart

Title:

Who

What

When

Where

Why

Solutions Master 17:
5W Chart

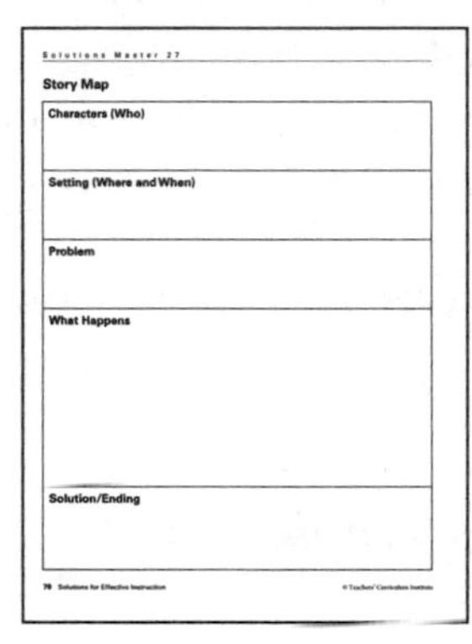
Story Map

Characters (Who)

Setting (Where and When)

Problem

What Happens

Solution/Ending

Solutions Master 27:
Story Map

Beginning-Middle-End Chart

Beginning

Middle

End

Solutions Master 28:
Beginning-Middle-End Chart

Drafting Strategies

Move from Organizer to Draft

Demonstrate how to move from the graphic organizer to the draft. For example, display a completed Venn diagram on transparency. Point to the title and tell students that it is the topic of your paragraph. Then point to the overlapping section of the Venn diagram, and tell students that they can use the ideas here to write their first sentence or two about how the two things are like. Then explain that their next sentence or sentences will be about how the two things are different, and point to the outer parts of the Venn diagram. Model writing the draft from the organizer, making clear connections from organizer part to paragraph part.

Present Sentence Starters

Write sentence starters on the board that are appropriate to the type of writing assigned. Model completing them.

Comparison

____ and ____ are alike in many ways. First, both____ and ____...

Contrast

____ and ____ are different in many ways. First, ____..., but ____ ...

Description

The ____ looks like ... It has ____... Sounds of ____ come from it.

Cause and Effect

First, ____ happened. That caused ____. As a result, ____.
Because of ____ ,...

Narration/Steps in a Process

First, ____. Next (Second), ____. Later, (Then) ____. Finally,
(Last, At last), ____...

Identify Paragraphs

Write a sentence from the text or based on the text on the board or on a transparency. Sketch horizontal and vertical lines that resemble the lines of lined paper around it to emphasize how the sentence begins at the left margin. Write a brief paragraph next to it, from the text or based on the text, and also sketch lines of lined paper around it. Ask students to name the similarities, such as the following: *Both are written from top to bottom and left to right; both leave spaces between words; both begin with a capital letter and end with a period. Both state at least one complete idea.* Ask students to name differences. *The paragraph is longer; it is indented; it tells more; it is made up of sentences.*

Variation Project *Solutions Master 1: Venn Diagram* and use it to compare and contrast a sentence and a paragraph.

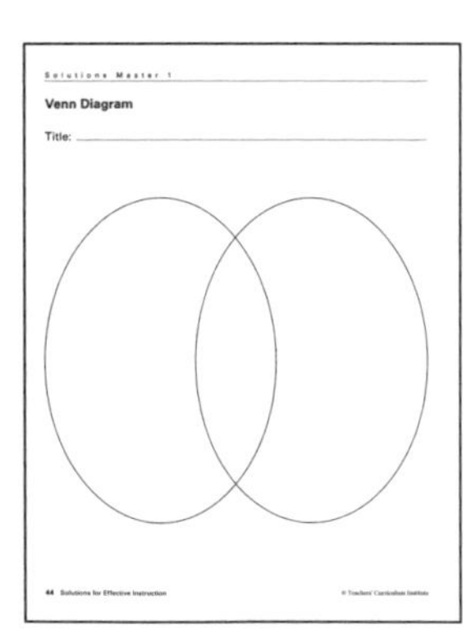

Solutions Master 1:
Venn Diagram

Revising Strategies

Read Aloud

Have students read their work aloud to a classmate. Encourage them to listen for what sounds right and for the flow of ideas. Ask them to say what they do or do not understand or follow.

Engage in Peer Feedback

Have students work in pairs or small groups to help each other revise. Project *Solutions Master 29: We Help Each Other Write* and explain or elaborate on, as needed, each of the checklist items. Distribute a copy of the list to each student. Ask students to refer to it when engaging in the feedback process.

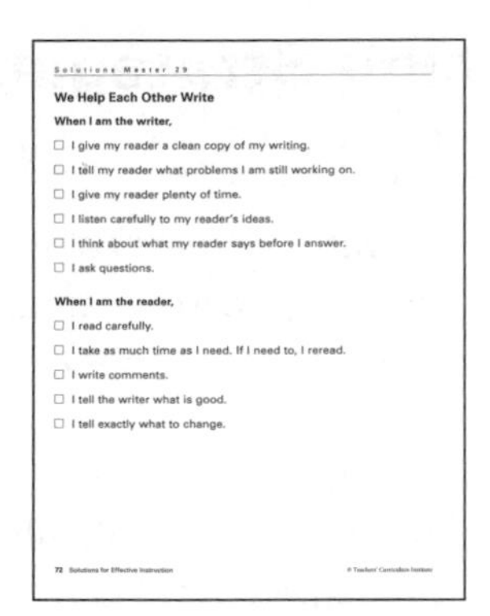

Solutions Master 29

We Help Each Other Write

When I am the writer,

- ☐ I give my reader a clean copy of my writing.
- ☐ I tell my reader what problems I am still working on.
- ☐ I give my reader plenty of time.
- ☐ I listen carefully to my reader's ideas.
- ☐ I think about what my reader says before I answer.
- ☐ I ask questions.

When I am the reader,

- ☐ I read carefully.
- ☐ I take as much time as I need. If I need to, I reread.
- ☐ I write comments.
- ☐ I tell the writer what is good.
- ☐ I tell exactly what to change.

72 Solutions for Effective Instruction © Teachers' Curriculum Institute

Solutions Master 29:
We Help Each Other Write

Add Describing Words

Before students revise, review describing words. Remind students that they tell color, size, shape, and other details about how things look. They also tell how things taste, smell, feel, or sound. Describing words can also tell how, how much or how many, when, and where. Model how you might add describing words to a sentence about your family or to a sentence related to a topic on which students are writing.

Link Words with Visuals

If students have added visuals to their writing, have them ask themselves:

- Will my reader know why this picture/chart/other visual is here?
- Do I need a title?
- Do I need a caption?
- Do I need a sentence that introduces the visual?

Use an Editing and Proofreading Checklist

Distribute copies of *Solutions Master 30: My Editing and Proofreading Checklist.* Teach or review checklist items as needed. Ask students to use the checklist to judge and change their writing.

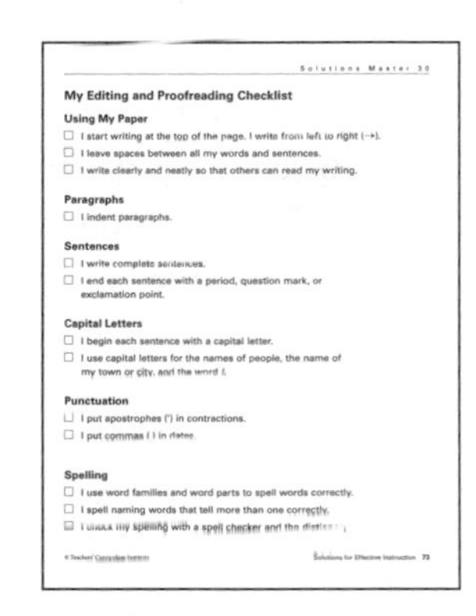

Solutions Master 30

My Editing and Proofreading Checklist

Using My Paper

- ☐ I start writing at the top of the page. I write from left to right (→).
- ☐ I leave spaces between all my words and sentences.
- ☐ I write clearly and neatly so that others can read my writing.

Paragraphs

- ☐ I indent paragraphs.

Sentences

- ☐ I write complete sentences.
- ☐ I end each sentence with a period, question mark, or exclamation point.

Capital Letters

- ☐ I begin each sentence with a capital letter.
- ☐ I use capital letters for the names of people, the name of my town or city, and the word *I*.

Punctuation

- ☐ I put apostrophes (') in contractions.
- ☐ I put commas ( ) in dates.

Spelling

- ☐ I use word families and word parts to spell words correctly.
- ☐ I spell naming words that tell more than one correctly.
- ☐ I [illegible] my spelling with a spell checker and the [illegible]

© Teachers' Curriculum Institute Solutions for Effective Instruction 73

Solutions Master 30:
My Editing and Proofreading Checklist

Publishing Strategies

Create Covers

Encourage students to create colorful and interesting covers. Use ideas for titles and bylines to review correct capitalization of titles and names. Remind students that titles and cover art should reflect the topic.

Create a Gallery Walk

Post or display writing assignments in the classroom. Give students time to walk around the room and read. Then, as a class, discuss students' reactions to the Gallery Walk.

Create Classroom Books

Gather student work on the same topic into classroom books. Divide the class into four small groups and give each group one of these tasks:

- alphabetize the work by title or author
- create a table of contents
- create an index
- title the work, create a cover, and bind the "book"

Make a Class Web Page

Create a Web site or add a page to your class Web site for social studies writing. (Your school IT professional may need to upload it to the net for you or link it to other school pages.) Use it to publish writing as well as to further a concrete sense of audience among your student writers.

Speaking and Listening Strategies

Give and Follow Directions

Have pairs of students use their completed copies of *Solutions Master 13: My Social Studies Chapter* to take turns giving and following directions for finding or identifying chapter parts. Model a one-step direction for kindergarten, a two-step direction at grade 1, and a three- or four-step direction at grade 2:

Examples
Kindergarten Point to the name of the chapter.

Grade 1 Open your book to page 3. Name the social studies words.

Grade 2 Find the chapter part that comes at the end of the Chapter 1. Look for a box. Tell me what's in the box.

Solutions Master 13:
My Social Studies Chapter

Discuss New Words

Project *Solutions Master 18: Word Rating Chart,* and talk about how familiar students already are with new vocabulary terms. Invite students to talk about where they have heard the words before or what they think they mean. Use the chart to sum up the class's knowledge. Return to the chart to talk about how their knowledge of the word has changed after students read the chapter and do the activities.

Solutions Master 18:
Word Rating Chart

Use a KWL Chart

Project *Solutions Master 14: KWL Chart,* and have students articulate what they know and what they want to learn about the topic they will read or hear about. After reading or listening, complete the chart by discussing and recording students' oral reflections.

Solutions Master 14:
KWL Chart

Use Text Structure Graphic Organizers

Have students work together to summarize aloud the content of graphic organizers they used to take notes during reading or to generate and/or organize ideas for writing.

Alternatively, help students complete graphic organizers such as a sequence chart, main ideas and details chart, cause-and-effect diagram, or whatever is appropriate to the topic, as they listen to you read a section of the text aloud or as they listen to other oral reports or sources of information.

"Read" Illustrations

Have students work together to summarize aloud what one or more of the chapter illustrations show. Encourage them to use social studies words and describing words.

Example *The children are busy playing. They are happy. They are smiling. Some children are talking, and some are listening. Some are taking turns.*

Describe People, Places, and Things Using Illustrations

Have students use describing words to tell what the illustrations show. As needed, provide sentences starters such as

The people look...

The school/building/teacher/ town has...

The homes/buildings are...

Read-Pair-Share

1 Have students read sections of the chapter on their own.

2 Pair students. Have them discuss what they read in an open-ended way, or assign something to identify orally, such as a sequence, a problem and solution, a main idea, or a cause and effect.

3 Have one member of the pair report to the class.

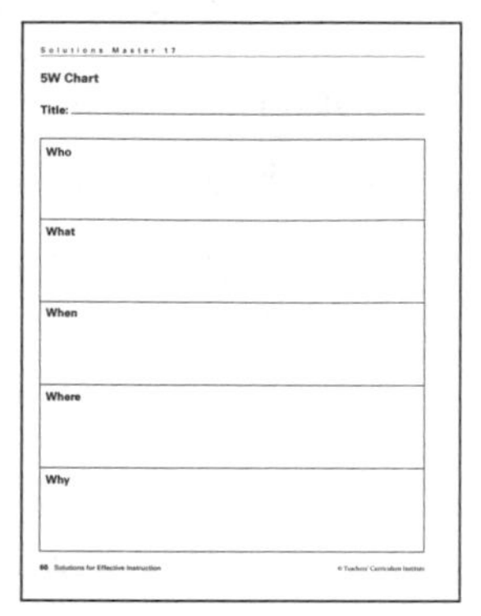

5W Chart

Title:

Who

What

When

Where

Why

Solutions Master 17:
5W Chart

Paraphrase Oral Information

When you orally introduce or sum up a chapter or section, have students work in pairs to paraphrase what you said.

Variations

- When students give oral reports, have listeners paraphrase what they heard.
- When students act as each other's peer readers during the writing process, have the writer paraphrase the feedback given by his or her reader.

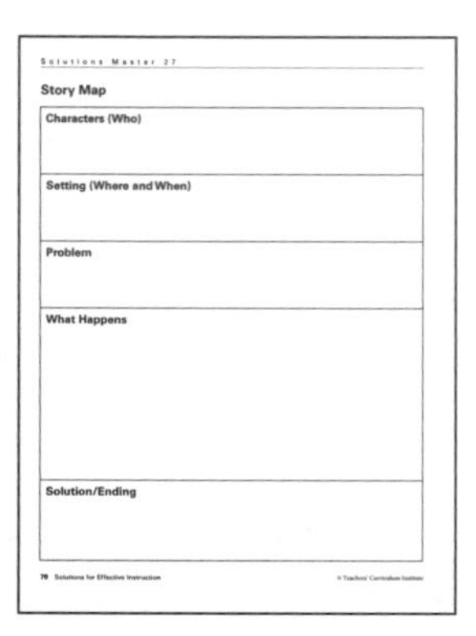

Story Map

Characters (Who)

Setting (Where and When)

Problem

What Happens

Solution/Ending

Solutions Master 27:
Story Map

Recite, Retell, Paraphrase

Use Reading Further sections as opportunities to teach, model, and have students practice the oral skills of reciting, retelling, and paraphrasing.

Examples

Kindergarten Students can recite the full names of family members and their relationship to the student (based on pages 11–12); students can retell the events shown by the pictures on pages 23–24; students can paraphrase the information on pages 41–44.

Grade 1 Students can paraphrase "A Place to Share," pages 8–9; retell "The Ant's Lesson," page 19; or recite school rules (based on pages 28–29).

Grade 2 Students can retell the events or nonfiction story on pages 8–11; they can paraphrase the information on all or part of pages 20–23; they can recite facts about the life of George Washington Carver or a list of products he developed (based on pages 58–61).

Optional Extension Have students use a *Solutions Master 17: 5W Chart, Solutions Master 27: Story Map,* or *Solutions Master 28: Beginning-Middle-End Chart* to help them plan before retelling a narrative. Have students use a main idea and details organizer or other organizer for expository text to help them plan before paraphrasing information.

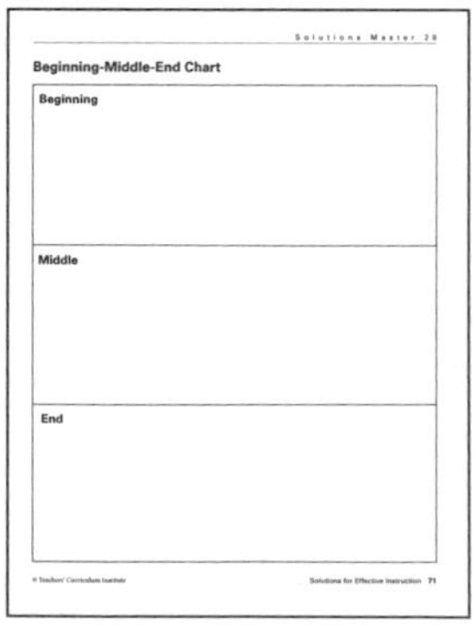

Solutions Master 28:
Beginning-Middle-End Chart

Sketch Ideas

1 Encourage students to draw, diagram, or sketch what they hear.

2 Ask students to use their sketches to explain or tell the main idea of what they heard.

Solutions Master 31

My Speaking Checklist

Before I Speak

- ☐ I plan what I will say.
- ☐ I write what I will say.
- ☐ I practice out loud.
- ☐ I listen to feedback.
- ☐ I revise and practice again.

As I Speak

- ☐ I stand or sit straight and tall.
- ☐ I look at my listeners.
- ☐ I use complete sentences.
- ☐ I try not to talk too fast or too slow.
- ☐ I speak loud enough for all to hear me.
- ☐ I show that I am interested in my topic by the look on my face.
- ☐ I pause between main ideas or events.
- ☐ I point to any pictures, maps, or charts I use. I do not stand or sit in front of them.

After I Speak

- ☐ I listen carefully to questions and comments.
- ☐ I answer questions and comments slowly and clearly.
- ☐ I think about ways to do better next time.

74 Solutions for Effective Instruction

Solutions Master 31: My Speaking Checklist

Listen for Patterns of Organization

Have students listen to a paragraph or section as you read aloud from the text. Have them tell what kind of organizer they should use for taking notes.

Examples

- Read a paragraph that compares and contrasts; lead students to request a Venn diagram.
- Read a paragraph that presents ideas and explains or supports them; lead students to request a support chart or a web.

Create Oral Practice with Vocabulary

Have students use social studies words to tell about the pictures in their chapters or sections.

Variation Have students use social studies words to ask questions about the pictures in their chapters or sections.

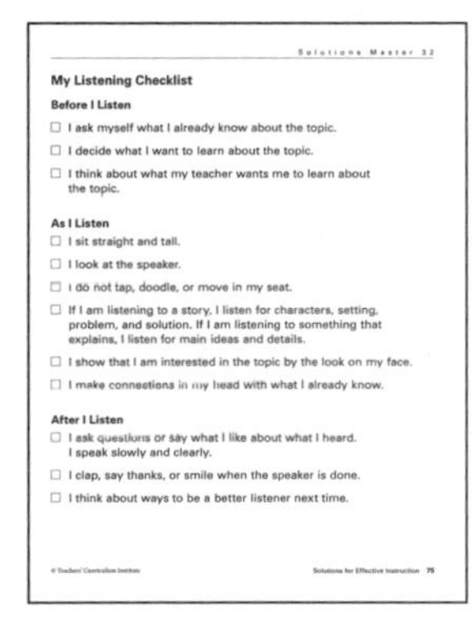

Solutions Master 32

My Listening Checklist

Before I Listen

- ☐ I ask myself what I already know about the topic.
- ☐ I decide what I want to learn about the topic.
- ☐ I think about what my teacher wants me to learn about the topic.

As I Listen

- ☐ I sit straight and tall.
- ☐ I look at the speaker.
- ☐ I do not tap, doodle, or move in my seat.
- ☐ If I am listening to a story, I listen for characters, setting, problem, and solution. If I am listening to something that explains, I listen for main ideas and details.
- ☐ I show that I am interested in the topic by the look on my face.
- ☐ I make connections in my head with what I already know.

After I Listen

- ☐ I ask questions or say what I like about what I heard. I speak slowly and clearly.
- ☐ I clap, say thanks, or smile when the speaker is done.
- ☐ I think about ways to be a better listener next time.

Solutions for Effective Instruction 75

Solutions Master 32: My Listening Checklist

Use a Speaking Checklist

Distribute copies of *Solutions Master 31: My Speaking Checklist* to help students plan for and reflect on formal speaking occasions.

Use a Listening Checklist

Distribute copies of *Solutions Master 32: My Listening Checklist* to help students plan for and reflect on formal listening occasions.

Part Three

Differentiating Instruction

Best Practices for English Language Learners

English language learners are those students in our classrooms whose native language is not English. No matter how capable, creative, and motivated these students are, their developing language skills can interfere with their academic success. The following best practices help address issues related to English language learners and support student success in the general education classroom.

Set up your classroom for success

- Establish a classroom environment in which students feel safe to answer questions, share ideas, and volunteer for classroom activities.
- Develop and state consistent classroom routines.
- Display pictures and charts to support content.
- Create a word wall that includes key vocabulary, definitions, and pictures.
- Identify language goals as well as content goals for your lessons.
- Incorporate materials that reflect diversity.

Build additional background knowledge (schema) to help students connect to content

- Use a visual, illustrated story, or short dramatic role-play to build background knowledge, preview the lesson, and elicit personal responses.
- Help students make connections with their personal experiences.

Pre-teach vocabulary

- Present vocabulary practice activities that incorporate multiple learning styles.
- Encourage the use of flashcards.
- Include words, definitions, and pictures on your classroom word wall.
- Allow students to use dual language dictionaries as needed to understand new vocabulary.

Teach understanding of concepts and big ideas

- Model and encourage the use of a method such as concept mapping for organizing content around big ideas.
- Provide frequent repetition.
- Use concept mastery strategies based on providing examples and non-examples and have students build the definition of a concept.

- Support the teaching of content with sketches, diagrams, and other visuals.
- Integrate social studies content into language arts instruction and vice versa.

Develop fluency

- When students give a one-word answer, model elaboration, or ask for elaboration, depending on the student's level of proficiency.
- Have students paraphrase what other students say.
- Provide multiple opportunities for pair-share and small group discussion before sharing in a large group.
- Structure classroom procedures so that all students regularly have the opportunity for oral participation.

Provide support for the text

- Teach students how to read the text using built-in text supports (glossary, chapter summaries, etc.).
- Model how chapter features (chapter title, section headings, the summary, etc.) provide you with a content overview and assist you with locating information.
- Model and emphasize looking at text in small, manageable sections.
- Highlight and annotate key vocabulary for other reading materials, such as primary sources, trade books, or other supplemental texts.

Organize information to support understanding of content

- Model how to use graphic organizers to record information.
- Present new information in a format that organizes and summarizes ideas, such as a chart or diagram.
- Have students draw or find visuals that will make content more understandable to them.

Assess frequently

- Check for understanding throughout the lesson.
- Create assessments that ask students to demonstrate their learning in ways that call on a variety of abilities (for example, drawing a picture, writing a poem, creating a rap).
- Show models of finished products prior to product completion.
- Use an exit ticket or question-of-the-day strategy to make sure students are getting important content.
- Brainstorm as a class or group for ideas that can be incorporated into products.
- Provide students with choices about how they would like to demonstrate learning.
- Assess progress on individual lessons instead of relying only on a test at the end of a chapter.

Find ways to create a strong school-home connection

- Provide opportunities for students to share work with parents and elicit parental feedback.
- Invite parents to class to see how instruction supports student learning and how parents can reinforce learning at home.
- Send home important information in the languages of your students.
- Provide meeting times with parents that can fit their schedules.

Best Practices for Students with Special Needs

Learners with special needs are those students in our classrooms who have learning and/or behavioral disabilities that interfere with their academic success or who struggle with basic learning tasks required at this grade level. Some of these students have Individualized Education Plans (IEPs) that specify the modifications required in the general education classroom. The following best practices include modifications to help foster academic success.

Set up your classroom for success

- Display pictures and charts to support content.
- Use flexible grouping to make sure that special education students have the opportunity to work with learners of different abilities.

Purposely set expectations for, and connect with, your students

- Find ways that are unrelated to academic ability to highlight what these students do well.
- Establish clear and consistent rules and classroom procedures so students know what to expect each day.
- Help students create a system for staying organized throughout the day (notebooks, homework folder, daily assignment planner, etc.).
- Provide opportunities for special needs learners to be recognized in front of their peers for achievement.

Check your lesson plan for preview, activity, and process

- Include a preview for each lesson that will connect to the student, as well as set a purpose for learning.
- Check for understanding throughout, as well as at the end of, a lesson by using a think-pair-share strategy or having students repeat in their own words important ideas from the lesson.

Use multiple modalities (oral, visual, kinesthetic) to deliver content

- Give information about assignments and class content both orally and in writing.
- Support content with experiential activities and visuals to foster understanding.
- Reinforce content through multiple activities using different learning styles.

Organize each lesson around a powerful graphic organizer

- Use diagrams and charts.
- Create graphic organizers with visuals that provide a structure for students to connect with content.

Modify student handouts and reading assignments

- Photocopy text pages and highlight key content.
- Identify page numbers on assignments that help students locate information more efficiently in the text.
- Create cloze assignments that allow students to fill in missing words instead of writing lengthy answers.
- Reduce the number of items that need to be completed.

Allow alternative methods of demonstrating understanding

- Offer choice in products that involve different intelligences (writing assignments, artistic assignments, technology assignments).
- Group students to allow special education students to complete products with other learners.
- Provide alternative assignments for assessment, such as writing a postcard instead of a letter or drawing a poster instead of writing a composition assignment.
- Provide extended time for product completion as needed or dictated by the student's IEP.

Adapt chapter tests

- Provide a word bank.
- Underline key clue words in question stems.
- Eliminate one of the choices on a multiple-choice test.
- Refer to a student's IEP for test modifications such as reading aloud.

Find ways to create a strong school-home connection

- Contact parents frequently.
- Share positive comments prior to concerns when talking with parents.
- Provide parents with suggested strategies to support student learning.

Best Practices for Enrichment

Enrichment is appropriate for those students in our classrooms who master content at a more rapid pace than their peers do, as well as for students who find the content of particular chapters especially engaging. Enrichment opportunities should provide different work, not just more work: no matter how highly capable, creative, and motivated these students may be, they still rely on their teacher to facilitate meaningful learning. The following best practices help support students who are ready for enrichment opportunities.

Pre-assess knowledge

- Check what students know before a lesson and then teach beyond that knowledge.

Compact the curriculum

- Have students spend their time on meaningful activities rather than working with content they already know.
- Make sure the content is covered but allow for enrichment, such as having an anchor activity for all and then having students extend learning by studying the topic from another perspective, at the next step in the process, or at a higher level of thinking.

Vary text and resources

- Provide students with supplementary texts at multiple levels, including trade books and primary sources.
- Share TCI Enrichment Readings and other Online Resources for delving into content in greater depth.

Spiral discussions to lead to higher level questioning

- Purposefully develop questions at all levels on Bloom's taxonomy during the course of a lesson (that is, ask recall questions as well as questions requiring application, analysis, and synthesis).

Group students flexibly

- Within a heterogeneously grouped classroom, allow students who are ready for enrichment to work together.
- Structure groups in various ways, such as by interest, topic, ability, or student-selected groupings.
- Keep groups fluid, based on specific instructional needs.

Incorporate multiple learning styles into your classroom

- Ensure that students can use their strengths, talents, and interests in various areas to access information and demonstrate their learning.

Use tiered assignments

- Create assignments at multiple levels to meet the needs of diverse learners. These assignments should meet lesson goals but also ensure that all learners are engaged in meaningful, challenging work.

- Present varied levels of instruction based on the content presented, the process by which students learn content, and the products students create to demonstrate learning.

Provide independent project opportunities

- Allow students who are ready for enrichment opportunities to complete independent study work of greater breadth and depth than what is being presented to other students.
- Set up learning centers offering project choices, starter ideas, and resources.

Apply content to other areas

- Help students make connections to other topics and disciplines (for example, when learning about their school, students might read or make graphs using data about their school or classroom, or they might read a novel set in a school in which some issue about rules or correct behavior is the theme or central to the theme).

Maximize opportunities for students to understand what they have to learn rather than what they already know

- Make students aware that undertaking enrichment activities is a positive opportunity to learn more.
- Students ready for enrichment should not always be assigned to serve as tutors to students needing support.
- While students ready for enrichment may be able to work more independently, they still need their teacher to provide insights and guidance, as well as instruction in various tasks and activities, such as organization, study skills, locating resources, and taking notes.

Part Four

Solutions Masters

Venn Diagram

Title: ______________________________

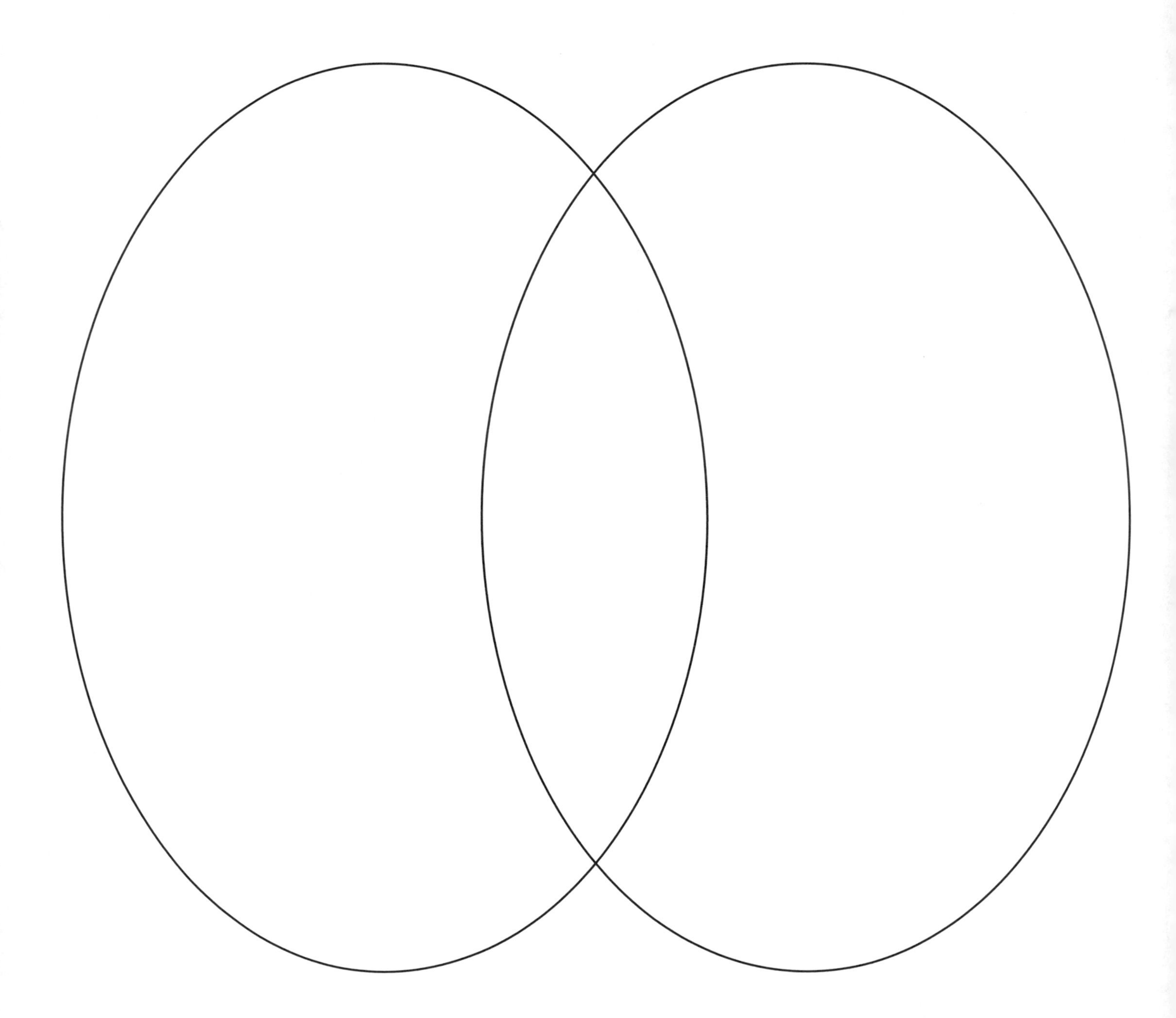

Two-Column Chart

Sequence Chain

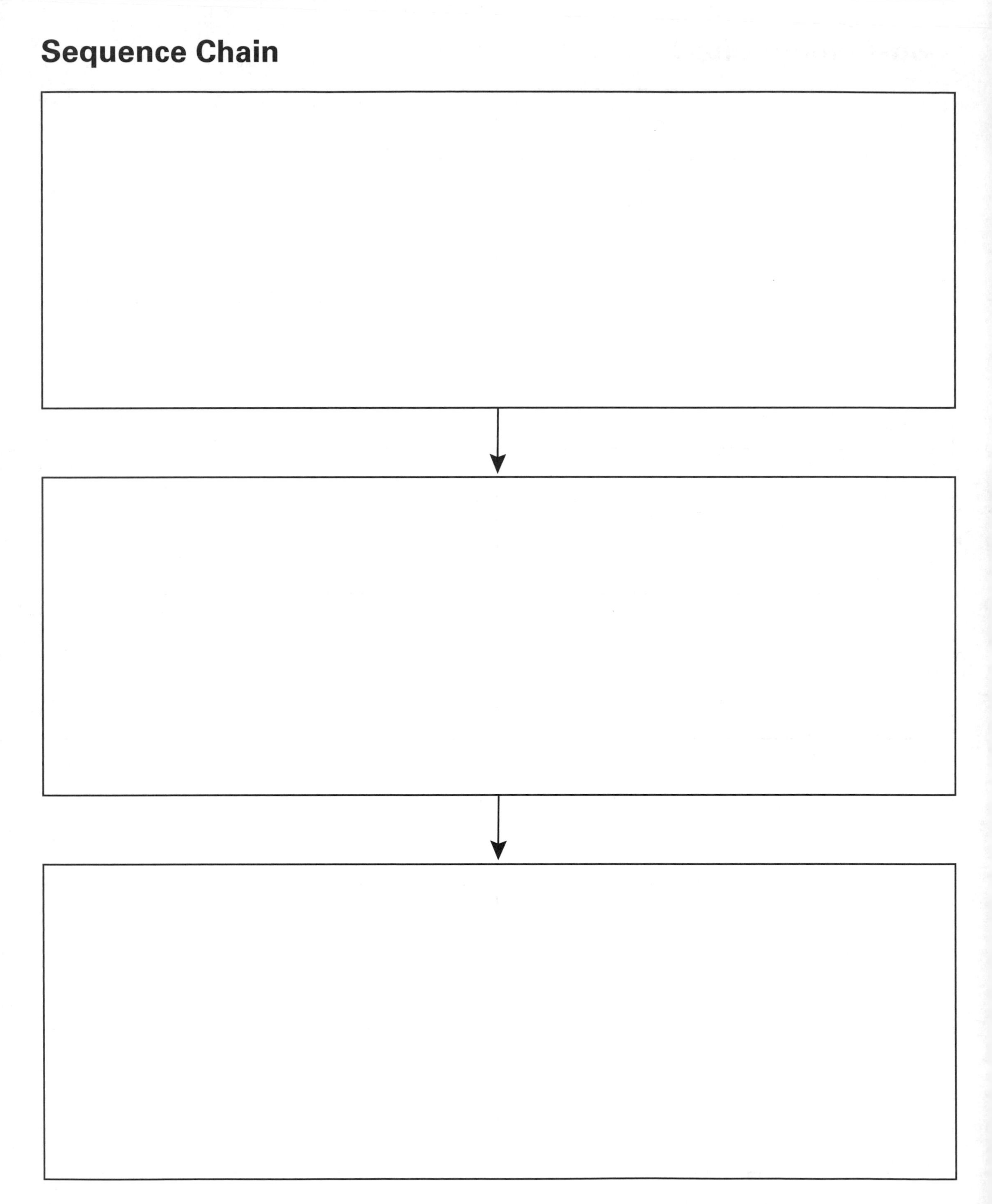

Cause-and-Effect Diagram

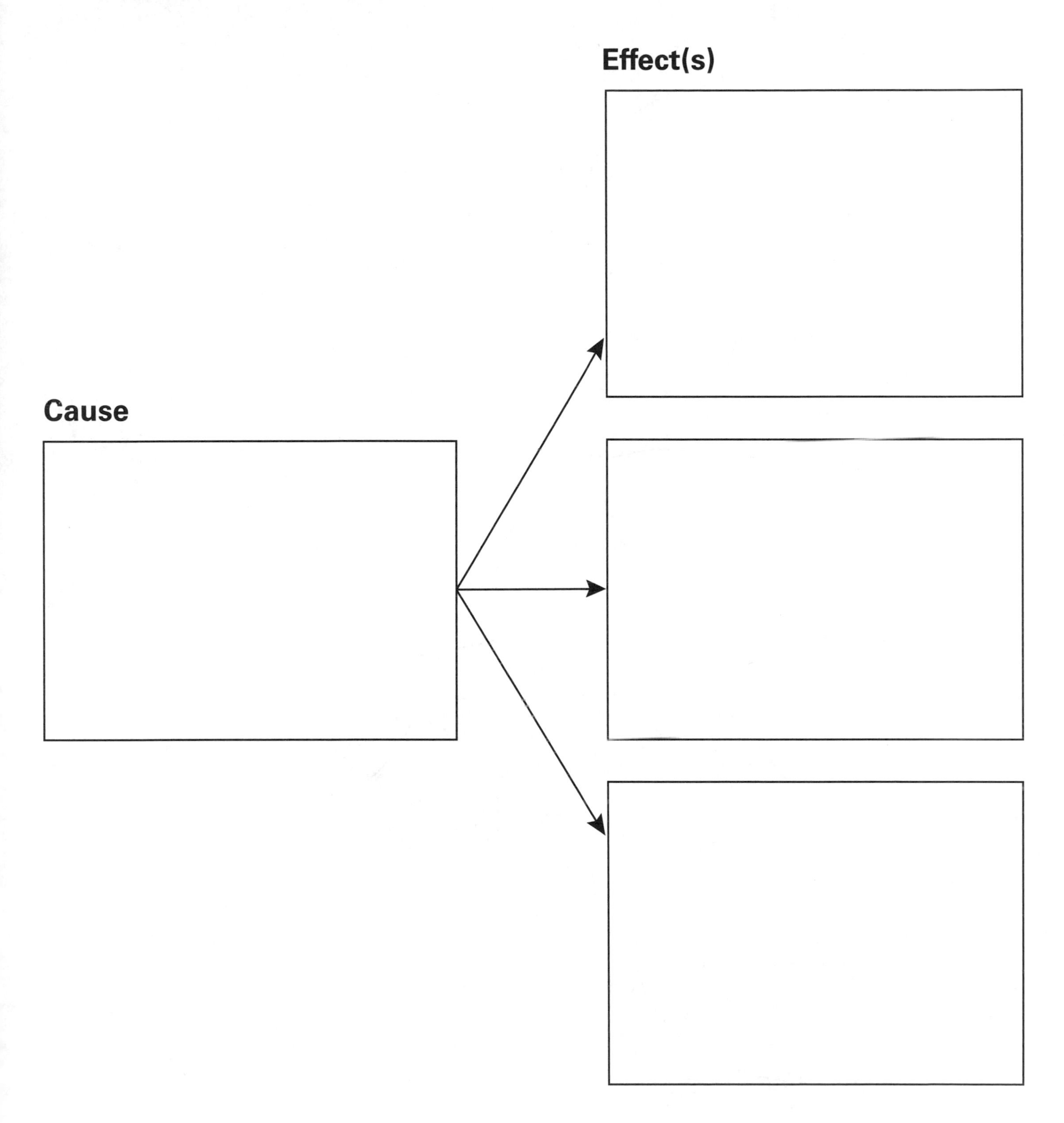

Web

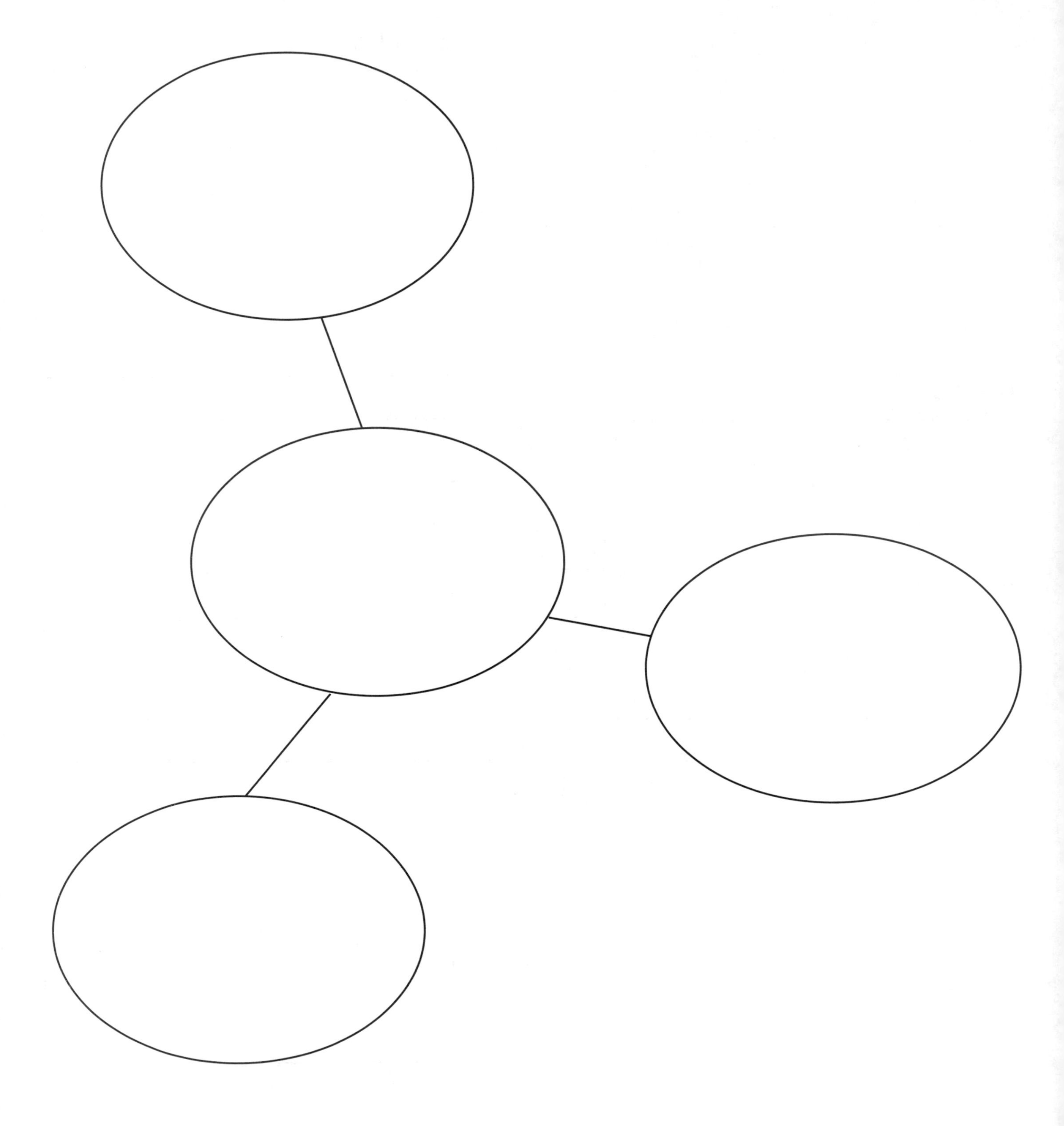

Prediction/Inference Diagram

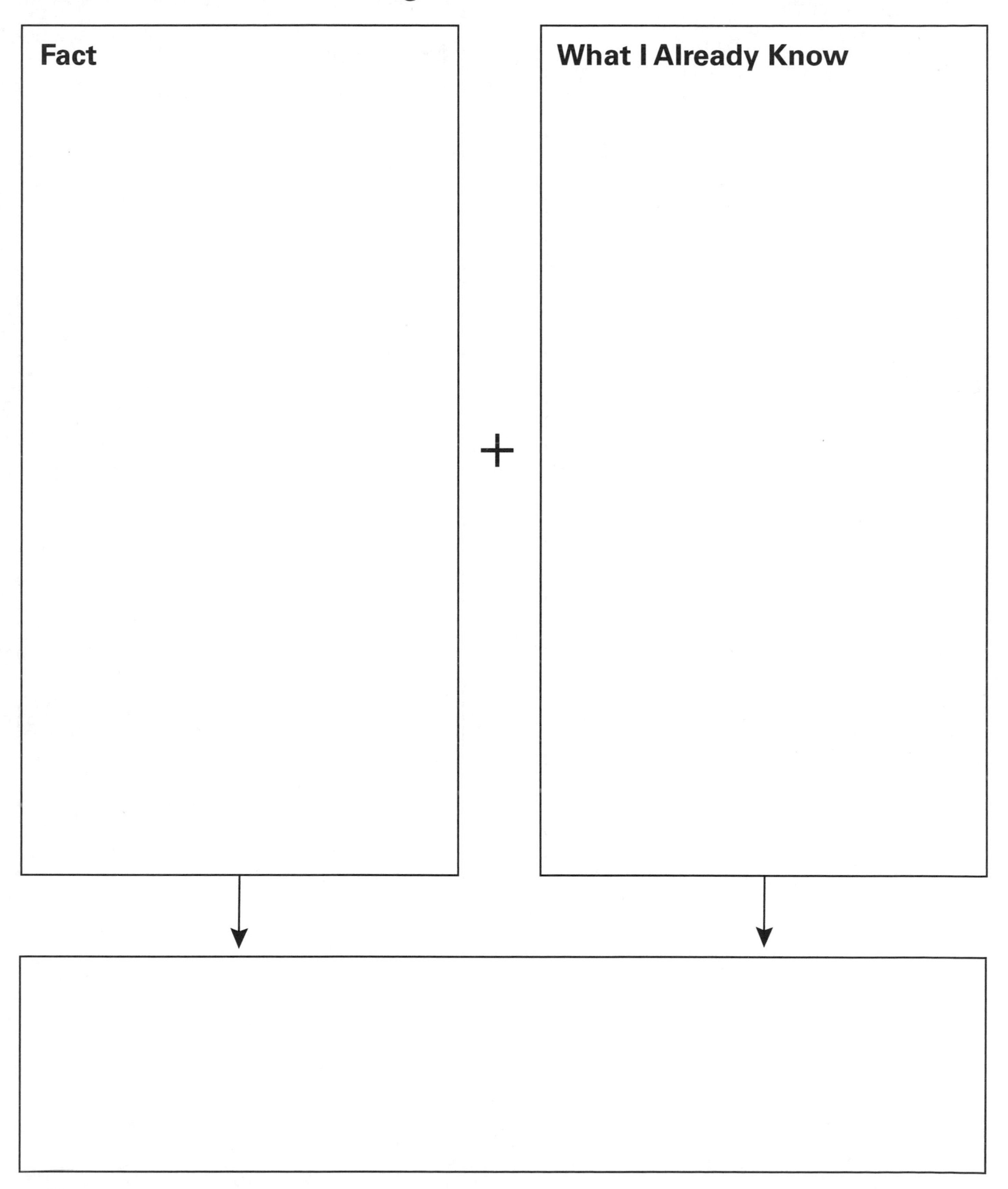

Draw-a-Conclusion Diagram

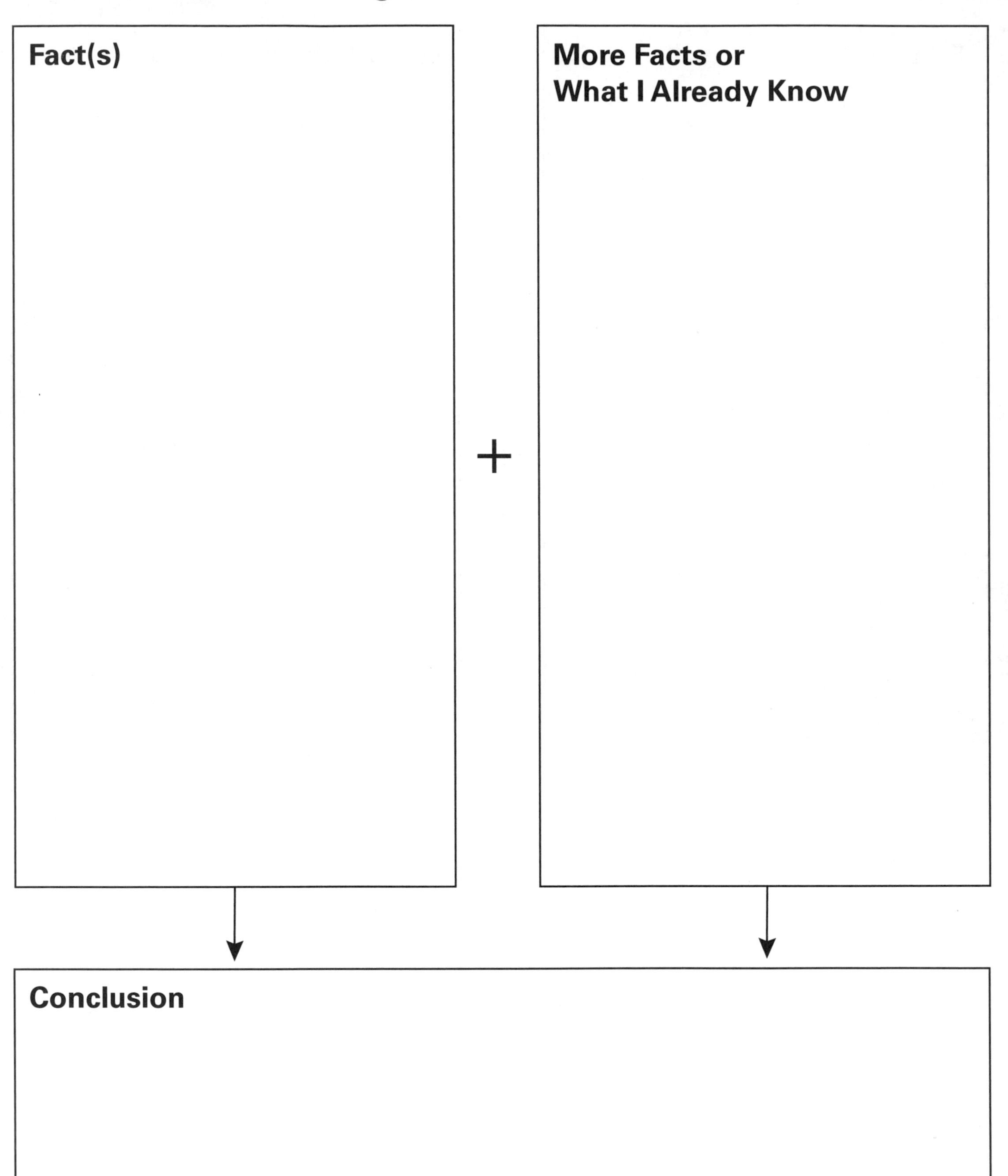

Summary and Generalization Diagram

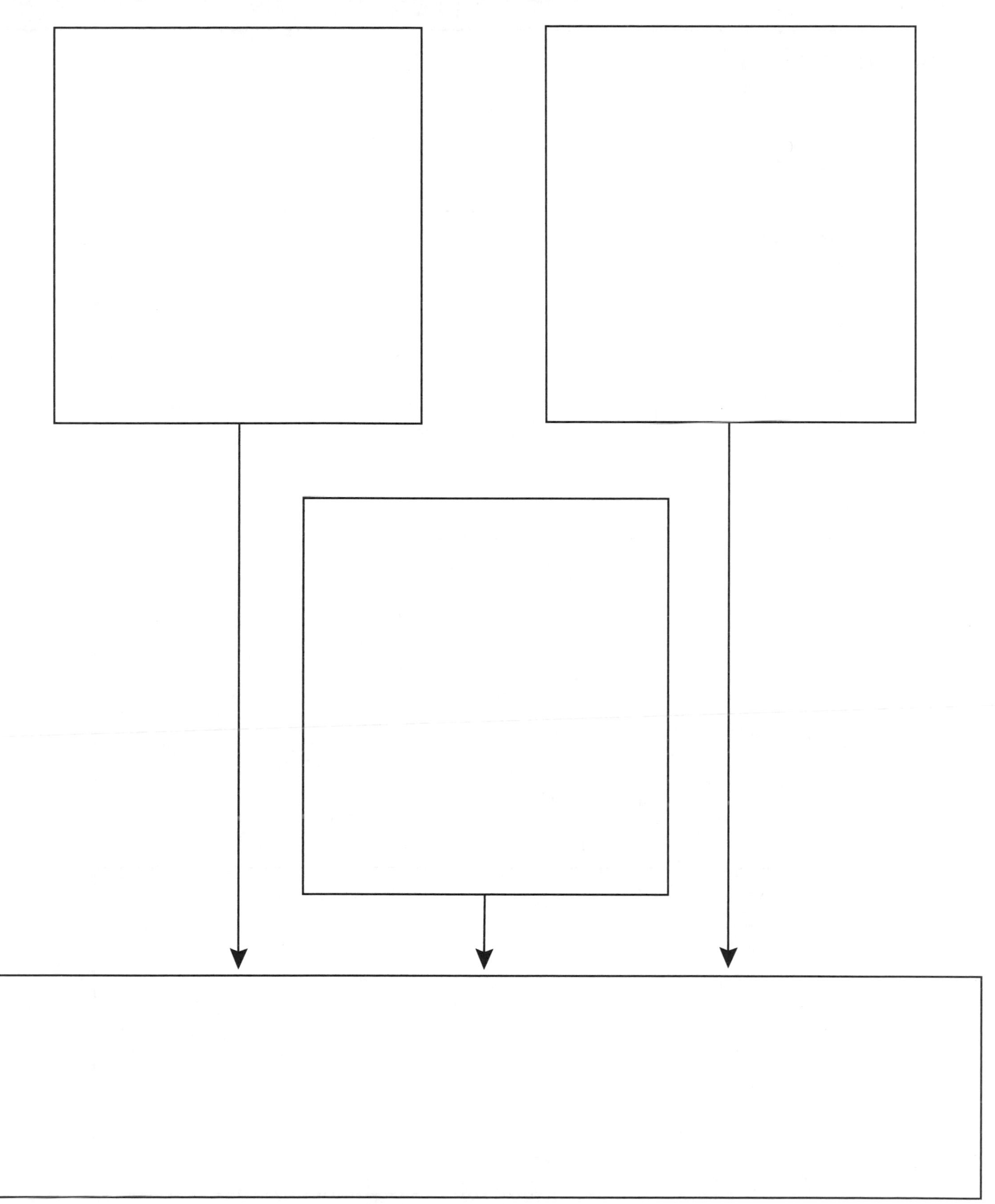

Support Chart

Opinion or Main Idea

Support

Support

Support

Decision Tree

Goal: ______________________________

Choices: ____________________ **or** ____________________

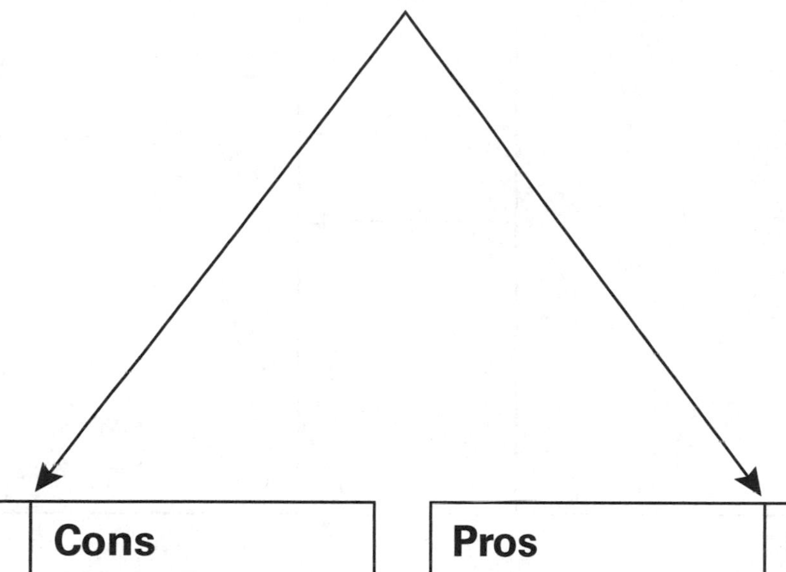

Pros	Cons

Pros	Cons

Decision

____

Flowchart

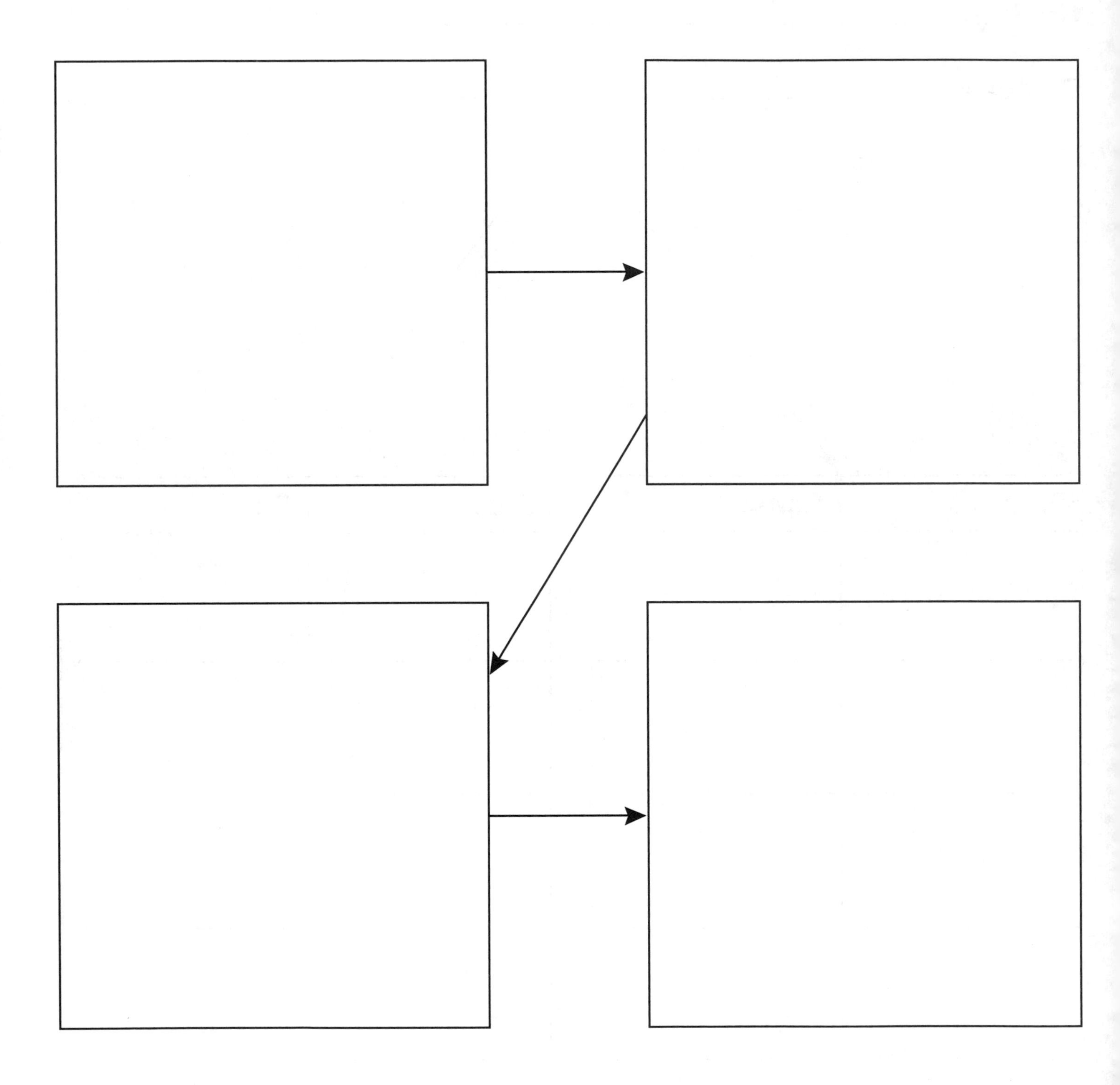

Timeline

Title: ______________________________

My Social Studies Chapter

Beginning	Middle	End

KWL Chart

I already know . . .	I want to learn . . .	I learned . . .

Make Connections Chart

In my book . . .	In my life . . .

Three-Column Chart

5W Chart

Title: ______________________________

Who
What
When
Where
Why

Word Rating Chart

Word	Know it well	Know it a little	Don't know it

My Word Parts Log

Social Studies Word	Prefix	Meaning of Word

Social Studies Word	Root	Meaning of Word

Social Studies Word	Suffix	Meaning of Word

Word Web

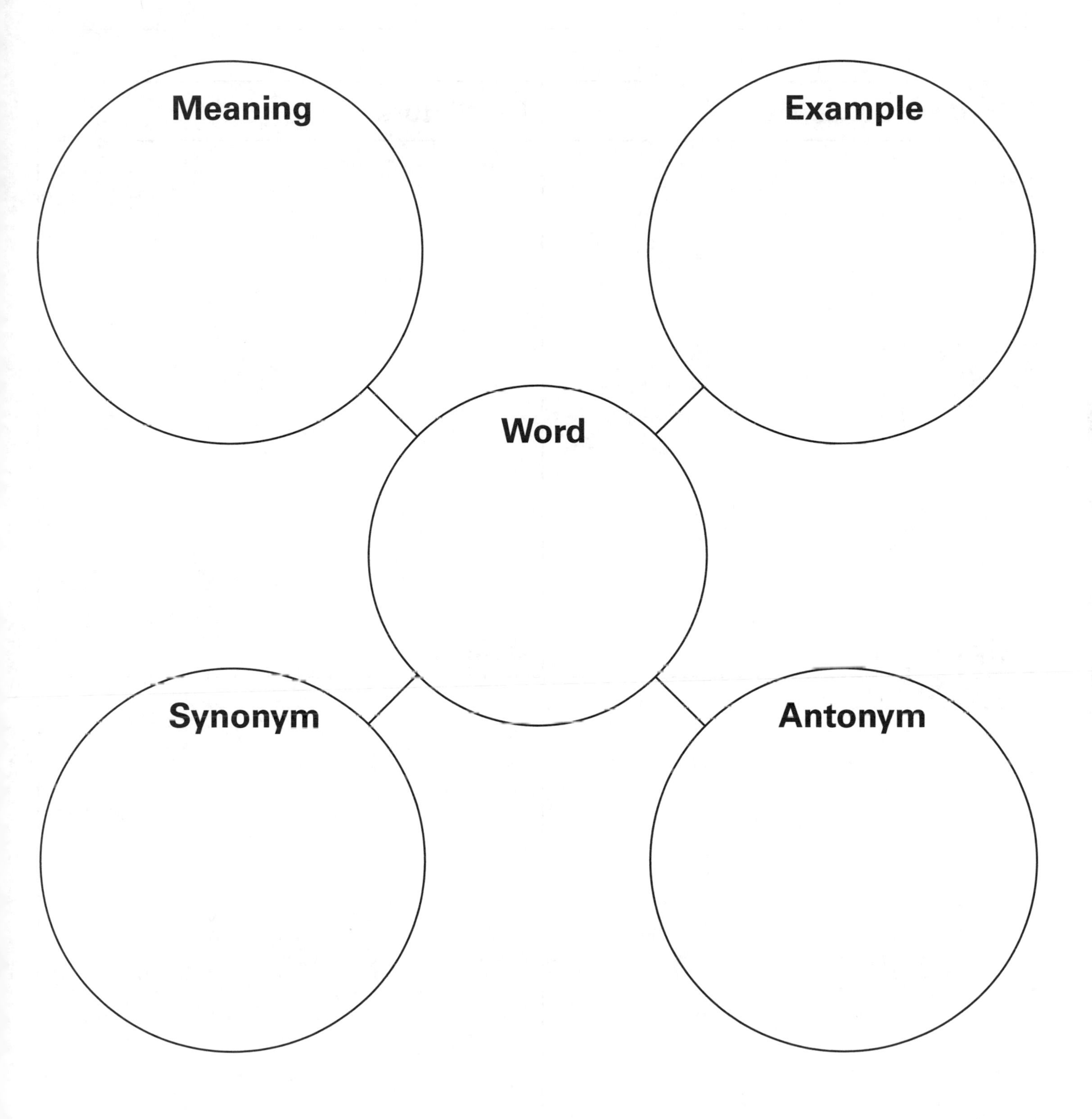

Word Map

Word: ______________________________

Context Sentence	My Picture

My Sentence	Definition

Word Wheel

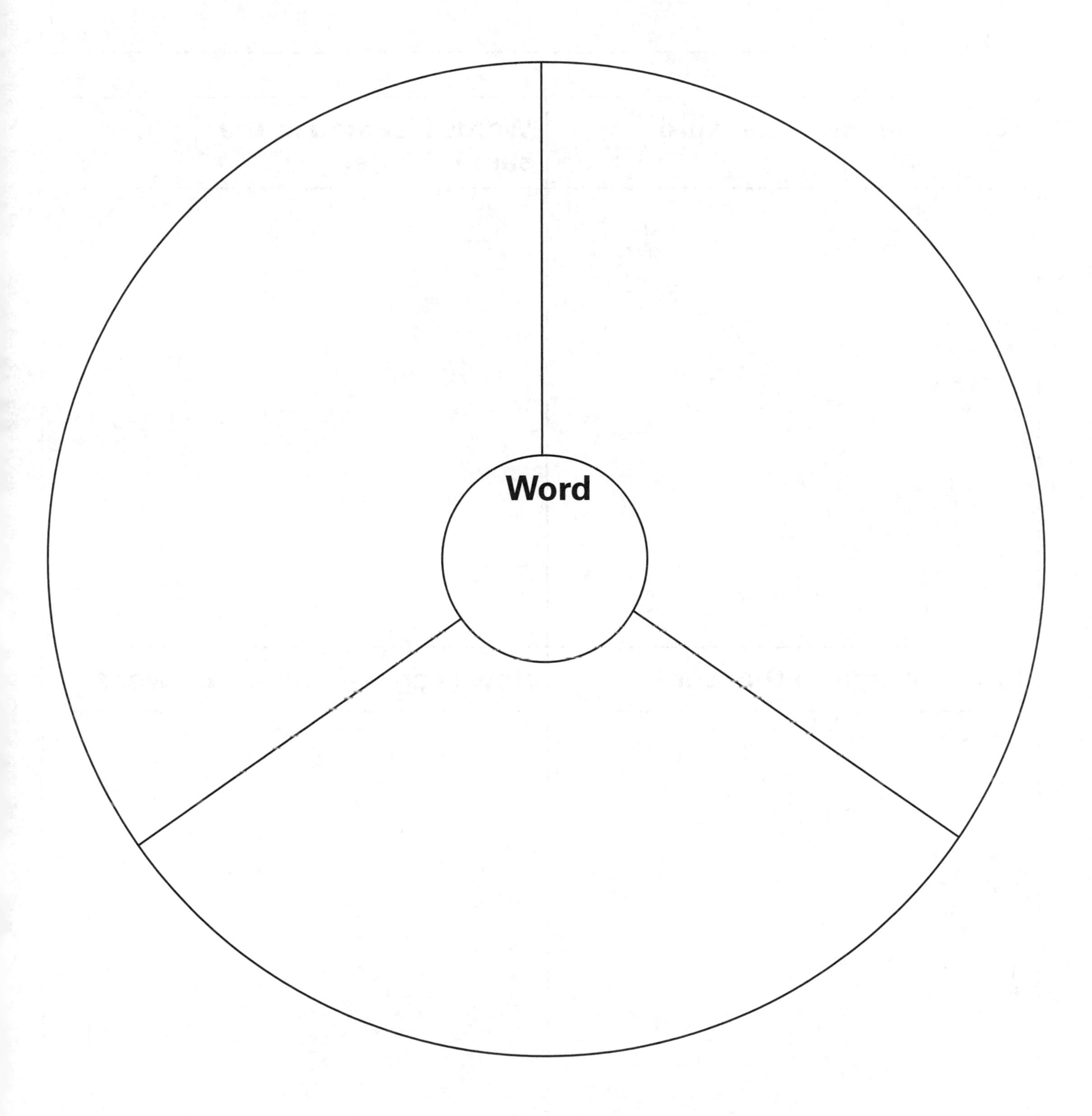

Getting to Know a Word

Word: ______________________________

Where I learned the word	Words I learned in the same chapter
How I could use the word	**How I can remember the word**

My Writing Process Checklist

Before Writing

- ☐ I think of ideas before I write.

Writing

- ☐ I tell about my ideas so that an adult can write them down.
- ☐ I use pictures to show my ideas.
- ☐ I use letters and words to tell my ideas.
- ☐ I form letters correctly.
- ☐ I leave spaces between words.
- ☐ I spell new words by using their sounds.
- ☐ I use sentences to tell my ideas.
- ☐ I sometimes use a computer to help me draw and write.

Revising

- ☐ I read my work to others.
- ☐ I make changes.
- ☐ I check my work.

Publishing

- ☐ I share my writing.

My Writing Process Checklist for Explaining or Describing

Prewriting

- ☐ I think about my reader.
- ☐ I choose one topic or main idea to write about.
- ☐ I ask myself, "What am I writing?" Then I choose and fill in a graphic organizer for that kind of writing.
- ☐ I put my ideas in an order that makes sense.

Drafting

- ☐ I begin in an interesting way and state my topic.
- ☐ I start new paragraphs for each new main idea and explain the main idea.
- ☐ I use my textbook or other sources to check my information.
- ☐ I use transition words to connect words and sentences.
- ☐ I sometimes add pictures, maps, or charts to make my meaning clearer. I make sure to tell about them in my writing.

Revising

- ☐ I reread my work to be sure the meaning and ideas are clear.
- ☐ I make changes by adding, taking out, or moving ideas.
- ☐ I meet with my teacher or a classmate to talk about my writing.
- ☐ I make more changes by adding, taking out, or moving ideas.
- ☐ I add words that describe.
- ☐ I read a classmate's writing and give helpful ideas for making it better.
- ☐ I use the editing and proofreading checklist.

Publishing

- ☐ I make a final, clean copy of my writing.
- ☐ I share my work.

My Writing Process Checklist for Stories, Steps, or Events

Prewriting

- ☐ I write down a list of ideas.
- ☐ I think about my reader.
- ☐ I choose one main idea to write about.
- ☐ I use a story map, flowchart, or beginning-middle-end chart to make a writing plan.

Drafting

- ☐ I begin in an interesting way. For a story, I tell the time and place.
- ☐ I start new paragraphs when the time, place, or speaker changes or for each new event or step in a process.
- ☐ I use words such as *first, next,* and *last* to connect words, sentences, and paragraphs.
- ☐ I sometimes add pictures to make the story or steps clearer.

Revising

- ☐ I reread my work to be sure I tell what happens in order.
- ☐ I make changes by adding, taking out, or moving ideas.
- ☐ I meet with my teacher or a classmate to talk about my writing.
- ☐ I make more changes by adding, taking out, or moving ideas.
- ☐ I add words that describe.
- ☐ I read a classmate's writing and give helpful ideas for making it better.
- ☐ I use the editing and proofreading checklist.

Publishing

- ☐ I make a final, clean copy of my writing.
- ☐ I share my work.

Story Map

Characters (Who)
Setting (Where and When)
Problem
What Happens
Solution/Ending

Beginning-Middle-End Chart

Beginning
Middle
End

We Help Each Other Write

When I am the writer,

- ☐ I give my reader a clean copy of my writing.
- ☐ I tell my reader what problems I am still working on.
- ☐ I give my reader plenty of time.
- ☐ I listen carefully to my reader's ideas.
- ☐ I think about what my reader says before I answer.
- ☐ I ask questions.

When I am the reader,

- ☐ I read carefully.
- ☐ I take as much time as I need. If I need to, I reread.
- ☐ I write comments.
- ☐ I tell the writer what is good.
- ☐ I tell exactly what to change.

My Editing and Proofreading Checklist

Using My Paper

- ☐ I start writing at the top of the page. I write from left to right (→).
- ☐ I leave spaces between all my words and sentences.
- ☐ I write clearly and neatly so that others can read my writing.

Paragraphs

- ☐ I indent paragraphs.

Sentences

- ☐ I write complete sentences.
- ☐ I end each sentence with a period, question mark, or exclamation point.

Capital Letters

- ☐ I begin each sentence with a capital letter.
- ☐ I use capital letters for the names of people, the name of my town or city, and the word *I*.

Punctuation

- ☐ I put apostrophes (') in contractions.
- ☐ I put commas (,) in dates.

Spelling

- ☐ I use word families and word parts to spell words correctly.
- ☐ I spell naming words that tell more than one correctly.
- ☐ I check my spelling with a spell-checker and the dictionary.

My Speaking Checklist

Before I Speak

- ☐ I plan what I will say.
- ☐ I write what I will say.
- ☐ I practice out loud.
- ☐ I listen to feedback.
- ☐ I revise and practice again.

As I Speak

- ☐ I stand or sit straight and tall.
- ☐ I look at my listeners.
- ☐ I use complete sentences.
- ☐ I try not to talk too fast or too slow.
- ☐ I speak loud enough for all to hear me.
- ☐ I show that I am interested in my topic by the look on my face.
- ☐ I pause between main ideas or events.
- ☐ I point to any pictures, maps, or charts I use. I do not stand or sit in front of them.

After I Speak

- ☐ I listen carefully to questions and comments.
- ☐ I answer questions and comments slowly and clearly.
- ☐ I think about ways to do better next time.

My Listening Checklist

Before I Listen

- ☐ I ask myself what I already know about the topic.
- ☐ I decide what I want to learn about the topic.
- ☐ I think about what my teacher wants me to learn about the topic.

As I Listen

- ☐ I sit straight and tall.
- ☐ I look at the speaker.
- ☐ I do not tap, doodle, or move in my seat.
- ☐ If I am listening to a story, I listen for characters, setting, problem, and solution. If I am listening to something that explains, I listen for main ideas and details.
- ☐ I show that I am interested in the topic by the look on my face.
- ☐ I make connections in my head with what I already know.

After I Listen

- ☐ I ask questions or say what I like about what I heard. I speak slowly and clearly.
- ☐ I clap, say thanks, or smile when the speaker is done.
- ☐ I think about ways to be a better listener next time.